Love on Mothers
Day 1979
Bruce, Merle
Jay & Vicki

Living Reliantly

Living Reliantly

A Devotional Study
of the 23rd Psalm

by

J. ALLEN BLAIR

LOIZEAUX BROTHERS
Neptune, New Jersey

CONTENTS

Contents

The 23rd Psalm

The LORD is my shepherd; I shall not want.

He maketh me to lie down in green pastures: He leadeth me beside the still waters.

He restoreth my soul: He leadeth me in the paths of righteousness for His name's sake.

Yea, though I walk through the valley of the shadow of death, I will fear no evil: for Thou art with me; Thy rod and Thy staff they comfort me.

Thou preparest a table before me in the presence of mine enemies: Thou anointest my head with oil; my cup runneth over.

Surely goodness and mercy shall follow me all the days of my life: and I will dwell in the house of the Lord for ever.

1.

THE PREPARATION

The Twenty-third Psalm is probably one of the most read and most appreciated portions in the entire Bible. Though written by David three thousand years ago, this short poem has never been improved upon or surpassed in any language. To our day it remains the sweet-singing nightingale of the soul, the majestic oak among the trees of faith, the Mount Everest of reliant devotion. What Handel's "Messiah" is to music, and Hunt's "Light of the World" is to art, the Twenty-third Psalm is to mankind.

Henry Ward Beecher wrote of this Psalm, "It has filled the air of the world with melodious joy, greater than the heart can conceive. It has charmed more griefs to rest than all the philosophy of the world. It has comforted the hearts of the poor. It has sung courage to the army of the disappointed."

The remarkable thing about the Twenty-third Psalm is that it is everybody's Psalm. The little child learns it at his mother's knee. The youth seeks its wisdom in hours of temptation and uncertainty. The aged quote it with quivering lips as the Angel of Death approaches. During all the years from childhood to old age, it is read and quoted repeatedly. Why? Because of its amazingly universal appeal.

Not only is the Twenty-third Psalm everybody's Psalm, but it meets everybody's need. Whatever the urgency or necessity, this Psalm assures us that if the Lord is our Shepherd, He will undertake. Am I famished in soul, depressed and discouraged? He provides rest and refreshing nourishment. "He maketh me to lie down in green pastures: He leadeth me beside the still waters." Have I committed sin and lost the joy of blessed fellowship with Him? If I confess, His mercy will prove sufficient. "He restoreth my soul." Does the future with its uncertainties confuse and perplex me? If so, I have surely forgotten all about His shepherding care. "He leadeth me in the paths of righteousness for His name's sake." Could it be that I am fearful of death and the life beyond the grave? What little faith! "Yea, though I walk through the valley of the shadow of death, I will fear no evil: for Thou art with me; Thy rod and Thy staff they comfort me." Do I become disturbed by those who, because of hate, seek to injure me by their deceitful tricks and unkind words? Why should I? He will not forsake me. "Thou preparest a table before me in the presence of mine enemies." Is there a sense of weakness and fruitlessness as I try to be a faithful witness for the Lord? There are no limits to His power. "Thou anointest my head with oil." Do I complain and grumble because of an envious heart? I must take time to count my blessings. "My cup runneth over." Do I look to failing self, and because of my own unworthiness, do I doubt my salvation and the assurance of Heaven? I need a greater vision of Him and less of myself. "Surely goodness and mercy shall follow me all the days of my life: and I will dwell in the house of the Lord for ever." Praise God! In Him, every need is met. The Twenty-third Psalm tells me so.

Assuredly the theme of this Psalm is "Living Reliantly." In portraying the dependent sheep following the Shepherd in his moment-by-moment watchfulness, the Psalmist reminds us of the necessity of constantly trusting our Great Shepherd's love for all things if we would continue on in the path of victory.

It is interesting to note, there isn't a single petition in the Psalm. It is a catalog of the mercies of God. Not once does the Psalmist ask or beg for anything. He rejoices repeatedly in God's gracious and abundant provision. He says triumphantly, "The Lord is my Shepherd; I shall not want." David knew all about the peaceful and happy contentment known only to those who fully trust in the Lord.

It is possible that you have read the Twenty-third Psalm many times, and yet, you may not have entered into the fullness of its meaning. Possibly you have memorized it, but do you know it *by heart*? Have its divinely-chosen words become a present reality in your life?

Before going any further, we should acquaint ourselves with the *preparation* essential for the complete understanding of the passage. Consider what precedes and what follows the Psalm. It is providentially placed in a most significant environment. Without experiencing the truth of the Twenty-second Psalm it is impossible to appropriate the blessings of the Twenty-third. The Twenty-second Psalm is well-known as "The Psalm of the Cross." In it we see numerous prophecies of the agony our Lord suffered in His crucifixion. The Psalm begins with the mystical question our Lord was heard to utter on the cross, "My God, My God, why hast Thou forsaken Me?" (Psalm 22:1) and ends with the solemn words, "He hath done this," which may also be translated, "It is finished." Throughout the Twenty-second Psalm we see the horrors of Mount Calvary descriptively and pictorially revealed.

Now look beyond the Twenty-third Psalm to the Twenty-fourth. Read through it and what do we see? It is unmistakably clear. This is "The Psalm of the King." There is no trace of the humiliated Saviour, but rather the Man of Glory who returns to earth to rule and reign in righteousness. "Lift up your heads, O ye gates; and be ye lift up, ye everlasting doors; and the King of glory shall come in. Who is this King of glory? The Lord strong and mighty, the Lord mighty in battle" (Psalm 24:7-8). As yet, this has not been fulfilled. But indeed it will be, when Christ returns to reveal His authority and power.

Now see the picture. Psalm Twenty-two looks to the past, presenting the *Good Shepherd* as the Saviour who was crucified for the sin of the world, proving His unlimited love. Psalm Twenty-four looks to the future, presenting the *Chief Shepherd* as the Sovereign who will return for His coronation. On one side of the Twenty-third Psalm we have Mount Calvary, on the other, Mount Zion. Nestled between these two great mountains of revealed truth we see the Twenty-third Psalm with its quiet, green valley and still waters, with the *Great Shepherd* gently and tenderly leading His sheep.

We are living in the "valley days." The Twenty-third Psalm is for today. It is a Psalm of new life and resurrection glory. For all who have believed on the Lord Jesus, the Psalm may be a present reality. All the promises are for believers.

But before going deeper into the rapturous truths of this wonderful Psalm, let there be no misunderstanding about the gate of entry. It is impossible to realize the joy of the Twenty-third Psalm without first of all going through the Twenty-second. What do I mean? Just this—you have no right to the promises of the Twenty-third Psalm until you recognize the redeeming work of Christ in the Twenty-second. Then realizing what He did for you, believe on Him as your living Lord. No one can know Christ's gracious and shepherding care until he knows Him as his Redeemer.

Some want to get to the Twenty-third Psalm without the Twenty-second. This is impossible! Before the Shepherd can care for the sheep, He must possess the sheep. The prophet Isaiah tells us, "All we like sheep have gone astray; we have turned everyone to his own way; and the Lord hath laid on Him the iniquity of us all" (Isaiah 53:6). Because of our sin we have shut ourselves out from the fold of God. But the way into the fold has been provided. The Lord Jesus is the Way. "The Lord laid on Him the iniquity of us all." Christ died on the cruel cross for your sin and mine. Indeed He is the "Good Shepherd," of whom we read in John 10:11, "the good shepherd giveth His life for the sheep." This is the truth of Psalm Twenty-two, Christ crucified. In Psalm Twenty-three we see Him as the living Lord, and indeed He is. He arose from the dead and longs to save and keep all who believe on Him.

But I repeat, it is absolutely impossible to receive the promises and blessings of God until you realize the sacrifice Christ provided for your sins. God has always demanded a blood sacrifice for sin. From Genesis to Revelation there is no scriptural truth more prominent than "salvation by blood." It began at the gates of Eden. After Adam and Eve transgressed God's law, the Lord appeared in His mercy and slew animals as a blood sacrifice for sin, using the skins as a covering for Adam's and Eve's naked bodies. This was a type of the covering for sin provided by the shed blood of the Lord Jesus.

Later we see Abel offering a blood sacrifice from "the firstlings of his flock" (Genesis 4:4). By this act of faith God numbered him among the believers according to Hebrews 11:4, "By faith Abel offered unto God a more excellent sacrifice than Cain, by which he obtained witness that he was righteous."

Little is said of the sixteen centuries following Abel's day, but the Scriptures do tell us of the flood. Because of sin, judgment came upon the earth and mankind was destroyed. God brought forth a new earth from this awful baptism of water. Notice the first recorded act after the waters subsided, the offering to God of a blood sacrifice. As soon as Noah left the ark, he built "an altar unto the LORD; and took of every clean beast, and of every clean fowl, and offered burnt offerings on the altar" (Genesis 8:20). Here was a new beginning for the world, but not without a blood sacrifice.

Again sin prevailed, and God laid an entirely new foundation for the establishment of His kingdom on earth. By means of the divine call of Abraham and the miraculous birth of Isaac, a new people was chosen to witness for Him. But this was not without a blood sacrifice. Abraham soon learned the meaning of this great truth as he willingly offered up Isaac. God provided the ram as a substitute. And Isaac, who was to die symbolically, rose from the dead, typical of the believer's resurrection in Christ. This again was not without a blood sacrifice.

We have touched on only a few of the events in the opening pages of the Bible. We might consider Israel's deliverance from Egyptian bondage by the blood of the paschal lamb sprinkled on the door frames; or the sprinkling of the blood first on the altar, then on the book of the covenant, and then on the people at Sinai as Moses declared, "the blood of the covenant" (Exodus 24:8); or the establishment of the Tabernacle where God was to dwell in the Holy of Holies and offerings of the blood sacrifices were to be made. But I want to hasten on to the New Testament.

Some think the message of a blood sacrifice for sin is for the Old Testament only. But what does the Bible say? There are scores of verses that teach just the opposite. I would like to choose just one incident from many. When John the Baptist saw Christ at the beginning of our Lord's earthly ministry, he made two declarations. They are most significant. First, he said, "Behold the Lamb of God, that taketh away the sin of the world" (John 1:29). The Lord Jesus was the perfect fulfillment of all the Old Testament sacrifices. He was to shed His blood for our sins. Secondly, John said that the Lord Jesus "is He that baptizeth with the Holy Spirit" (John 1:33).

The baptism of the Holy Spirit has to do with the placing of the sinner into a vital union with the Lord whereby he enters into the fellowship and enjoyment of the Living Christ, the truth of the Twenty-third Psalm. But there must be no mistake. Before the second promise can be received, the first must be believed. Christ must be received into the life as the one who suffered, bled, and died for our sins, the truth of Psalm Twenty-two. Christ must be seen as "the Lamb of God that taketh away the sin of the world."

Have you accepted the Lord Jesus Christ as your sacrifice for sin? If not, do so now, then enter into all the joys of the wonderful Twenty-third Psalm. Let the Lord truly be *your* Shepherd.

2.

THE PERSON

"The LORD *is my Shepherd"*

Many years ago Dr. Joseph Parker announced his Scripture reading as the Twenty-third Psalm. Slowly and distinctly he read, "The-Lord-is-my-Shepherd." There was a long pause. Then, closing his Bible he said, "That is enough!" That brief phrase so gripped his heart that he could read no further. Anyone who prayerfully considers the truth found in those five words will soon realize that here is the key to joyful and happy living. Why? Because they speak of the *Person* who is the source of all joy and happiness.

We should notice that the Psalm opens with "The LORD is my shepherd" and closes with "I will dwell in the house of the LORD for ever" (verses 1, 6). The "LORD" appears at the beginning and at the end of this majestic Psalm. How significant that in the last book of the Bible the Lord Jesus declares, "I am Alpha and Omega, the beginning and the ending" (Revelation 1:8).

One readily notices from the Psalm that not only is our Lord the beginning and the end, but all in between.

Exclude Him from this sublime passage and no longer will it be the "pearl of Psalms," but only an empty shell. The same is true of life. Without the Lord in our hearts we are nothing or have nothing. Life without Him is a hopeless blank. As sheep are dependent upon the shepherd, so we are dependent upon the Lord. Without the shepherd, sheep are completely helpless. They cannot find their way through the treacherous mountain passes or valley darkness, but the shepherd can. They are not strong enough to resist the attacks of wild and ferocious beasts, but the shepherd is. They will not lie awake throughout the night in watchfulness to protect themselves from possible dangerous foes, but the shepherd will. As sheep need a shepherd, so we need the Lord. "Without Me," Jesus said, "ye can do nothing" (John 15:5). Yet I have met many who felt they were all-sufficient without God. Facing the snares and pitfalls of unknown paths, they have tried in their limited wisdom and strength to find their own way. How foolish, when we have a Shepherd who loves us and longs to help us.

Before going further, it might be well to consider who the "Lord" is, whom David speaks about in this Psalm. You will recognize in the King James version of the Bible that "Lord" is printed in capital letters. In this form, it signifies "Jehovah," the eternally, self-existent One, who in Himself possesses all life, being a God of righteousness, holiness, and love.

Now skip along quickly over the pages of history

about one thousand years. We hear someone speaking. He stands only a few miles from the place where centuries before Jehovah had revealed Himself to Moses. Hear His words, "I am the good shepherd: the good shepherd giveth His life for the sheep" (John 10:11). Who is this? Why, the Lord Jesus Christ. David had declared, "The Lord is my Shepherd." Jesus said, "*I am* the Good Shepherd." Of whom then was David speaking? It can be no other than Jehovah—Jesus. Jesus of the New Testament is the Jehovah of the Old. F. B. Meyer writes of Him, "As Jehovah, He has all power; as Jesus, all sympathy. As Jehovah, He sustains all worlds; as Jesus, He ever liveth to make intercession. As Jehovah, He is sovereign Lord of all. As Jesus, He still treads the pathways of this world by our side, whispering sweetly and softly in our ears, 'Fear not, little flock'" (Luke 12:32).

What our Lord was to David, He is to us. Time cannot change Him. He is the Master of time, "The Lord *is* my Shepherd." As for David, so for you and me. Christ is forever the same, our immutable Lord, "Jesus Christ the same yesterday, and to day, and for ever" (Hebrews 13:8). Because "The Lord *is*," the entire Twenty-third Psalm becomes a present possession for anyone who believes on Him.

One time while reading the Twenty-third Psalm, a Christian stopped abruptly at the end of the third word —"The Lord *is*." "Why," he exclaimed, "that is the greatest fact in the universe." Who of us would doubt him? Indeed this is a tremendous truth. Not only is Jesus Christ existent today in the body at the right hand of God the Father, but He is in Himself everything. He *is* love. He *is* peace. He *is* grace. He *is* righteousness. "In Him dwelleth all the fulness of the Godhead bodily. And ye are complete in Him" (Colossians 2:9-10). All He is and all He possesses is ours, if we are His.

This blessedness can only be known as we enter into a personal relationship with Him. Salvation is an individual matter. Until we say, "The LORD is *my* Shepherd," we shall know nothing of the assurance of His eternal salvation. Regrettably, many must read the Psalm, "The LORD is *a* Shepherd." They cannot say, "*my* Shepherd," for they have not yet come to Him and believed on Him. It is one thing to speak of "*a* bank" but quite another to be able to say "*my* bank." I have a particular interest in the bank where I deposit my money. For me, it is "*my* bank." Who is the Lord Jesus Christ to you? Is He merely *a* Shepherd? Or can you confidently affirm with David, "The Lord is *my* Shepherd"? This little two-letter word "my" is the key that unlocks the door to God's best. It is the golden link that binds us to Christ forever. Thomas knew the Lord in a nominal way. He had lived and worked with Christ. But it was a long while after he met the Saviour before he could say, "*My* Lord and *My* God" (John 20:28).

You may ask, "How may one know definitely that he

belongs to God? Can we be certain that we shall be with Him after death?" Most assuredly, if you have entered the *door* of the sheepfold.

Several friends were traveling in Palestine. They reached a high ridge overlooking the village of Bethlehem. Seeing a sheepfold, they went in. In a few moments the owner appeared, a veteran shepherd.

"Is this your sheepfold?" asked one of the travelers.

"Aye," was the quick reply.

"And is this where the sheep sleep?" pointing to a rough shelter thrown up against the rock in a corner. The shepherd nodded.

"But there is no gate to the fold; how do you close the sheep in at night?" The old shepherd looked at the two travelers as though they should have known better.

"I am the door," he said assuringly. And gathering his loose robe tightly around his ankles, he was down in a moment, squatting in the doorway, his back against one post, his feet against the other, his knees drawn up and clasped by his weather-beaten hands. Gently he bowed his head and closed his eyes, as many a time he had closed them to catch a few hours sleep under the starlight.

"I am the door," he repeated again and again. "I watch the sheep throughout the night." Then he added with a note of triumph in his voice, "And I have never lost a lamb from my fold yet."

The Lord Jesus said in John 10:9, "I am the door: by Me if any man enter in, he shall be saved, and shall go in and out, and find pasture." The only way to possess salvation and security is through Christ. He is "the Door." Believe on Him. If you do, He will give everlasting life. He promises, "I give unto them eternal life; and they shall never perish" (John 10:28).

In further thinking of our LORD as the Shepherd of those who believe on Him, let us consider the Oriental shepherd and his many responsibilities in caring for his sheep. Early in the morning he had to lead them out of the fold into the pasture lands for nourishment. It was necessary to keep constant vigil for wild animals which might attack the sheep, or robbers that might try to steal them. At certain times during the day the shepherd had to take them to a quiet brook or stream where the sheep might drink without being frightened. In the evening they followed him back to the fold where they rested peacefully through the night under his watchful eye. There were times in the year when the shepherd had to deviate from his daily routine and lead his sheep many miles away from home, seeking new pasture lands. With them he endured the heat of the day and the cold of the night. If they suffered, he suffered also. If a lamb could not keep up with the flock, the shepherd carried him in his bosom, speaking words of comfort, as a mother to a child. If one of the flock wandered away and got lost, the shepherd had to seek him out, often risking his own life. Considering the shepherd's love and attachment to his sheep as he gently leads them under all circumstances, I think of our blessed Lord of whom Isaiah writes, "He shall feed His flock like a shepherd: He shall gather the lambs with His arm, and carry them in His bosom, and shall gently lead those that are with young" (Isaiah 40:11).

The Hebrew word for "shepherd" is a primitive root meaning "to tend a flock, to pasture it." The word came to have the general meaning of "to rule." It also expresses the connotation of "association with (as a friend)." All three meanings would apply to the shepherding care of the Lord Jesus Christ. With a shepherd's heart and a shepherd's eye He watches over His sheep. In His Almighty strength and power He rules them as their Lord. As the "friend that sticketh closer than a brother" (Proverbs 18:24), He guides and directs them in well-tried and divinely chosen paths.

Not only is the shepherd obligated to tend his flock, the sheep must obey and follow the shepherd. He will provide for them and protect them—but they must follow. Is not the same true for the child of God? Nothing is more important for the Christian than a sincere desire to obey and follow Christ. Deviation from the will of God results in misery. David knew all about this. The Bible records several sad episodes revealing David's failure to obey. He yielded to the lust of the flesh, rather than to the will of God. But oh, what gnawing grief! What anguish of heart! Hear David's own sorrowful description, "When I kept silence, my bones waxed old through my roaring all the day long. For day and night Thy hand was heavy upon me: my moisture is turned into the drought of summer" (Psalm 32:3, 4). Surely there is no satisfaction in disobedience. David soon realized this and cried out to the Lord, "Have mercy upon me, O God, according to Thy lovingkindness; according unto the multitude of Thy tender mercies blot out my transgressions" (Psalm 51:1). God forgave David and from that moment he wholly followed the Lord.

In John 10:4 we read, "And when He [the Lord Jesus Christ] putteth forth His own sheep, He goeth before them, and the sheep follow Him." What is it to "follow Him"? It is to die to self completely and to allow Christ to be the Lord of the life. It is to permit the "Great Shepherd of the sheep" to "make you perfect in every good work to do His will, working in you that which is well-pleasing in His sight" (Hebrews 13:20, 21). Are you the Lord's entire possession? If not, bow your head and surrender yourself completely to Him. Then without question you will be able to say, "The LORD is *my* Shepherd."

3.

THE PREDICTION

"I shall not want"

In the first verse of the Twenty-third Psalm David makes a startling *prediction* concerning himself and his future, saying, "I shall not want." The more I consider it, the more I am convinced that this is an amazing statement. For David was not thinking only of a day, a week, a month, or even a year. He actually meant "I shall *never* want."

How could he be so positive? You reply, "That's very simple. David was a wealthy man." He was wealthy in his old age, but he offers no hint that his wealth provided such confidence. In fact, just the opposite, for in Psalm 62:10 he alludes to the insecurity and uncertainty of riches, "If riches increase, set not your heart upon them."

In itself this brief statement of David's could be interpreted as sheer presumption or vain boasting. How does anyone know what tomorrow will provide? What do we know about the future? You see how ridiculous this could be. When you realize, however, what precedes the phrase, there can be no question as to its feasibility. David's assurance that every need of his life would be supplied was not contingent upon the abundance of his riches, the greatness of his power, or his ability to achieve, but solely on the principle that he belonged to the Lord. "The Lord is my shepherd." Because of this realistic relationship with God, David could say with boldness, "I shall not want."

How marvelous it is to know that in a world of confusion and darkness, the true believer in the Lord Jesus Christ can say, "I shall not want." It is the privilege of everyone who has entered into a personal experience with Christ as Lord to trust Him for all things. God promises in Romans 8:32, "He that spared not His own Son, but delivered Him up for us all, how shall He not with Him also freely give us *all* things?" God is to be trusted not for *some* things but for *all* things. Job cried out to the Lord, "I know that Thou canst do every thing" (Job 42:2). Though tested sorely, his unshakable faith was evidenced as he shouted, "Though He slay me, yet will I trust in Him" (Job 13:15).

Many believers talk about trusting the Lord, but few seem really to practice it. They trust God while all is well, but when confronted with adversity or shrouded in mystery, faith vanishes. They worry, fret, and complain, looking in every direction but up. How foolish! God tells us in Matthew 6:34, "Take therefore no thought for the morrow: for the morrow shall take thought for the things of itself." If you have truly believed in Christ for salvation, you are His possession. He will not forsake His own. In Psalm 34:10 He assures us that "they that seek the Lord shall not want any good thing." How ridiculous for those of us who belong to Him to doubt His unerring wisdom and providential care.

Has worry ever accomplished anything for you? I heard of someone who said he did find worry to be advantageous: the things he worried about never happened. Doubtless this could be said of most of our worries. But actually, worry in the believer is a denial of faith and the repudiation of the power and wisdom of God. There are no limits to God's ability to undertake for every occasion. He has graciously promised to care for all the needs of your life: "But my God shall supply all your need"—spiritual, mental, physical, financial or whatever it may be—according to His riches in glory by Christ Jesus" (Philippians 4:19). There are absolutely no boundaries to the scope of God's possessions. For this reason He can fulfill all His promises.

To realize fully God's abundance, we must trust Him wholeheartedly. As sheep reliantly trust the shepherd, so believers are to rely confidently upon God. We are told that even before they are in the fold for the night, sheep instinctively know that their shepherd has already planned for their grazing throughout the next day. They are confident he will lead them to the green pastures. How or where, they do not know. But they have learned from past experiences that his gracious care has always been for their well-being. They never worry. The Apostle assures us in the marvelous truth of Romans 8:28 that "all things work together for good to them that love God." Has there ever been a single occasion in your past when God in His love and mercy failed you? Why then do you worry? Take God at His word according to Psalm 37:4-5, "Delight thyself also in the Lord; and He shall give thee the desires of thine heart. Commit thy way unto the Lord; trust also in Him; and He shall bring it to pass."

Sheep are the most helpless of all animals and, naturalists say, the dumbest. But they know they need have no fear. With our burdened hearts and confused minds we need to learn this simple truth. Paul tells us in 2 Corinthians 5:7 to "walk by faith, not by sight." Problems and anxiety may deluge us, dim our vision, and like helpless sheep we may not be able to see far ahead, but the Shepherd is there. His eyes can see all things ."The eyes of the LORD run to and fro throughout the whole earth, to show Himself strong in the behalf of them whose heart is perfect toward Him" (2 Chronicles 16:9). Have faith! Don't worry! Worry chokes the life of faith. Freedom from worry is faith in operation. If you have committed your life to Christ, if He is your Shepherd, you have nothing to fear.

Though sheep have limited vision, God has compensated by giving them an acute sense of hearing. Their eyes may deceive them, but never their ears. Especially are they sensitive to their shepherd's voice. A writer tells of a traveler in Syria watching three shepherds whose sheep were being watered, all mixed in together. The traveler wondered how the shepherds would ever get the sheep separated. Soon one shepherd raised his hands to his mouth and called, "Men-ah!" the Arabic for "Follow me"; and immediately thirty sheep clambered up the hill after him. Not one of his sheep remained.

The Lord Jesus said in John 10:27, "My sheep hear My voice, and I know them, and they follow Me." We may not see ahead, but we can hear His voice. That is, if we take time to listen. Hurry, like worry, is the result of unbelief and a failure to trust God. Those who rush madly through the day, without taking time to wait on the Lord with prayer and Bible reading, will not hear Him. They cannot possibly know His will. They will wander and grope blindly through the day, lost to His shepherding care. He promises in Psalm 32:8, "I will instruct thee and teach thee in the way which thou shalt go: I will guide thee with Mine eye." He sees all the perils and pitfalls up ahead. That's why He says, "Wait on the LORD: be of good courage, and He shall strengthen thine heart" (Psalm 27:14). Don't run ahead without Him. Take time to wait. He is never in a hurry. God takes His time. We, too, must learn to wait. Many of the failures and disappointments we have suffered are the result of haste. Do not rush! Do not move until you hear His voice. Then, when you have heard His voice, follow Him! The result? You will not want. Every need will be met. Worry will be unknown.

I believe all worry in the believer's life is the failure

to accept fully the first part of Psalm 23:1, "The Lord is my Shepherd." But you reply, "I have believed on Christ, though I still worry." You have believed on Christ, but is He truly your Shepherd? Is He leading your life? And, are you following? Remember, the shepherd always leads his flock. In the morning when he calls them from the fold, he leads them, and throughout the day always stays before them.

One time a guide in Palestine had told his party of tourists that the shepherd always leads his flock. Later in the day they saw a flock of sheep with a man behind, driving them. One of the party said to the guide, "I thought you said that was never done."

"Correct," replied the guide, "let's inquire." Going to the man the guide asked why he, as a shepherd, was driving his sheep.

"Shepherd?" he replied, "I'm not a shepherd. I am a butcher driving the sheep to the slaughter."

You may be sure Christ will never "drive" you to do anything. He is a Shepherd who lovingly "leads" His sheep. He says in John 10:4, "And when he putteth forth His own sheep, He goeth before them, and the sheep follow Him." Twice in the Twenty-third Psalm David declares, "He leadeth me." Read between the lines. If God were leading, David must have at this point in his life been following. Indeed he was. Everything had been fully committed to the Lord—home, family, health, finances, old age. Everything was in the hands of his Shepherd. No wonder David could say, "I shall not want." Until everything is wholly surrendered to the Lord Jesus, we cannot say, "I shall not want." If there are any wants in your life at this moment, it is possible there has not been a full commitment.

One time a little girl was called on in Sunday School to quote Psalm 23:1. Standing, she said, "The Lord is my Shepherd, that's all I want." When the believer comes to the place where he can say without reservation," "The Lord is my Shepherd," he will then know deliverance from stress and worry. For when we love Christ wholeheartedly, there remains nothing to worry about. Every need will be met after our greatest need of a full commitment to Christ has been satisfied.

Is the Lord Jesus truly the Shepherd of your life? This should be your only care. God says, "Seek ye first the kingdom of God, and His righteousness; and all these things shall be added unto you" (Matthew 6:33). Put first things first and all else will find its proper place. When Christ is your Shepherd, all your wants will vanish. The poorest believer becomes unspeakably wealthy. God will provide.

For many years George Mueller had been known for his boundless faith and implicit confidence in God. Years ago he founded and directed a splendid orphanage in England. At times there were insufficient funds to carry on, but the Lord always responded to the humble entreaties of this consecrated servant. One day as Mr. Mueller sat down to breakfast with the children, he explained that they had no milk, but that they should go right ahead and thank God for the milk, because their Heavenly Father knew their need and would provide. As they prayed and thanked God for what they did not yet receive, someone knocked at the door. When the prayer was completed, Mr. Mueller answered and there stood a milkman who explained that his milk wagon was broken down in front of the orphanage and it was necessary to dispose of the milk. He offered it all to the orphanage absolutely free.

God does supply if we are in a right relationship with Him. He says in Psalm 34:9, "There is no want to them that fear Him." To "fear" God is to permit Him to direct in all things. It is reverently to trust His guidance and leadership under all circumstances. David could say as he approached the sunset years of his life: "I have been young, and now am old; yet have I not seen the righteous forsaken, nor his seed begging bread" (Psalm 37:25). God will never forsake the righteous.

Is Christ your Shepherd? Have you invited Him to come into your life? If you have, then you can make the same prediction David made, "The Lord is my Shepherd; I shall not want."

4.

THE PRESERVATION

"He maketh me to lie down in green pastures"

If one has sincerely believed on the Lord Jesus Christ, he may say with unshakable confidence, "The LORD is my Shepherd." From the moment the penitent sinner enters God's fold through faith in Christ, he may claim all the privileges of the unmistakable guidance and loving care of the Lord. The Shepherd will *preserve* His sheep over the hills of uncertainty and through the valleys of perplexity, and surely bring them home safely to be with Himself. David tells us in Psalm 145:20, "The Lord preserveth all them that love Him."

The Twenty-third Psalm presents in marked clarity many of the ramifications of the Great Shepherd's preservation of His own. David says, "He maketh me to lie down"; "He leadeth me"; "He restoreth my soul"; "Thou preparest a table before me"; "Thou anointest my head with oil"; ultimately He takes me to "the house of the LORD forever." Our Great Shepherd never ignores His tasks nor forgets His responsibilities. He faithfully watches over all who belong to Him. David made many mistakes. He was human. On one occasion he succumbed to the temptations of the flesh and wandered far from God. But the Shepherd sought him out and brought him back. David confessed to the Lord, and all was well again. Later, with a heart overflowing with gratitude and with renewed assurance of the Lord's sustaining grace, he prayed, "Thou art my hiding place; Thou shalt preserve me from trouble; Thou shalt compass me with songs of deliverance" (Psalm 32:7). Most assuredly, our Great Shepherd preserves His sheep.

The Oriental shepherd had many duties in caring for his flock, but one of his chief responsibilities each day was to take them to a good pasture. Very early before dawn, about four o'clock, he starts them out on the rougher herbage, leading on throughout the morning to the richer, sweeter grass where they enjoy the best pasturage of the day. By ten or eleven o'clock they are well aware of the stifling and torrid heat of the noonday sun. It is time to rest. But sheep are not always ready to rest when they should. So the shepherd must make them lie down. He gently taps his leading sheep on the head. Quickly they respond and others follow. Here under the shade of a great rock or a clump of bushes the sheep rest in the soft, lush grass. Unknown to them they are being prepared for the long trail homeward which often leads over dangerous and untried paths. The experienced shepherd can see far ahead, so he prepares the sheep with refreshing rest.

We are told in God's word to "rest in the Lord" (Psalm 37:7). We also read, "In quietness and in confidence shall be your strength" (Isaiah 30:15). But like foolish sheep, we are too busy to rest. We are so occupied with our work and pleasures that we have little time for rest. Repeatedly our Great Shepherd calls to us saying, "Come ye yourselves apart . . . and rest a while" (Mark 6:31). But our ears are dull of hearing. Madly and thoughtlessly we rush on to self-chosen pastures, finding food, but receiving little nourishment. The prophet describes us well in Haggai 1:6, "Ye eat, but ye have not enough; ye drink, but ye are not filled with drink." Our souls are famished, our bodies are tired, and our nerves are jaded. We cannot continue for long under these circumstances. Our Great Shepherd is mindful of this. And because He has pledged Himself to preserve His sheep, He must act. Soon He does. In His abounding lovingkindness, He "maketh" us "to lie down."

It is infrequently that God makes us do anything. Sometimes He must. If we are too occupied with secondary things to hear His voice, then we may feel the touch of the "rod" in gentle, but firm rebuke. Even though we are busy serving Him and trying to lead others to Him, we are not excused from spending time with Him. Too often, we are running to meetings and sponsoring programs while neglecting to spend time in quietness with the Lord. How unproductive and unsatisfying it is to try to serve Christ without His presence and power. There is so much wasted energy in Christian circles because of so little time being spent seeking God's leading. We are so busy "doing" that we have little time for "resting."

To be useful and effective for Christ, there must be frequent seasons of periodic rest in Christ. The body demands rest. Vigorous souls are not usually found in tired bodies. God created all of us with physical limitations. To ignore them or to exceed them may mean sorrow.

Very wisely, F. B. Meyer has written, "There must be pauses and parentheses in all our lives. The hand cannot ever be plying its toils. The brain cannot always be elaborating trains of thought. The faculties and senses cannot always be on the strain. To work without rest is like overwinding a watch. The mainspring snaps and the machinery stands still. There must be a pause frequently interposed in life's busy rush wherein we can recuperate exhausted nerves and lowered vitality. There is more permanence than many think in the commandment which bids us rest one day in seven."

The soul cries for rest even louder than our bodies. So often the needs of the body are respected while the soul is neglected. One day the body will perish and disintegrate into dust, but the soul will never die. Jesus asked in Mark 8:36 and 37, "What shall it profit a man, if he shall gain the whole world, and lose his own soul? Or what shall a man give in exchange for his soul?" Our Saviour taught repeatedly that the soul is of inestimable and eternal value. If we are to spend eternity with God after death, the soul must be brought in touch with

Christ during life. There is no second chance beyond the grave. It is urgent that we believe on Christ now.

Without the Lord Jesus in the life the soul is restless and totally ignorant of the peace and felicity of God. Isaiah tells us, "The wicked are like the troubled sea, when it cannot rest, whose waters cast up mire and dirt. There is no peace, saith my God, to the wicked" (Isaiah 57:20-21). Although God's peace may be unknown to him, the very moment one believes on the Lord Jesus he will enter the fold of God and be able to say with David, "This is my rest for ever: here will I dwell" (Psalm 132:14).

For those who have committed themselves to the Lord Jesus, the soul demands more than rest. It needs food. The word "pasture" as used in the Bible means "food" as well as "rest." To be mature and virile Christians, we must have spiritual food. We need to feed upon the Living Bread. The Lord Jesus declared, "I am the living bread which came down from heaven: if any man eat of this bread, he shall live for ever" (John 6:51). How do we feed upon Christ? By spending time in the "green pastures" of His Word, the Bible. Jeremiah was in the habit of spending much time feeding his soul on the Word. He confessed, "Thy words were found, and I did eat them; and Thy word was unto me the joy and rejoicing of mine heart" (Jeremiah 15:16). The Psalmist exclaimed, "How sweet are Thy words unto my taste! yea, sweeter than honey to my mouth!" (Psalm 119:103) Those of God's people, who give the first hour of the day to prayer and meditation in the Word, are the ones that shall derive the greatest blessing and shall be most extensively used in reaching others for the Lord. Emaciated Christians, habitually neglecting food for the soul, will have little effectiveness in the work of God.

Regrettably, many of God's people are carelessly "running" when they ought to be "feeding" and "resting." Failing to spend time with the Lord searching the Scriptures and listening to His voice, they are gradually getting spiritually weaker. To avoid the inevitable, our Great Shepherd must respond to preserve His sheep. Since we abuse our privilege and liberty "to lie down in the green pastures" voluntarily, our Shepherd makes it compulsory. We may not feel the need of spiritual rest and nourishment, but remember, we are only the sheep. The Lord Jesus is the Shepherd. There are many things the sheep do not know. The Shepherd knows all things. He is mindful of all our limitations and refuses to permit us to get too far from Him.

If we have strayed, it may be that we shall feel the gentle touch of His "rod" in a "light affliction, which is but for a moment," but "worketh for us a far more exceeding and eternal weight of glory" (2 Corinthians 4:17). Trials and afflictions should always prompt the believer to heart searching. Frequently I have known Christians to lament, "Why did God do this to me?" Let us not be quick to judge God. So often we bring sorrow on ourselves. God permits the sorrow to prevent us from wandering farther. The Lord's chastening is extremely beneficial. It always is. There are no exceptions. Is it not true that in the hour of trial we get closer to the Lord? We learn as never before what it means "to lie down in green pastures." David in analyzing his affliction said, "Before I was afflicted I went astray: but now have I kept Thy word. It is good for me that I have been afflicted; that I might learn Thy statutes" (Psalm 119:67, 71). He readily realized that his affliction was not brought on as a result of what he was doing, but what he was not doing. He had been neglecting to spend time with the Lord. When temptation came, he was too weak to resist.

Suppose we do not respond to the gentle touch of the "rod." Will our Great Shepherd forsake us in disgust and permit us to choose our own paths? Oh no, decidedly not! He cannot do this. We read His promise in Deuteronomy 31:6, "He will not fail thee, nor forsake thee." We are His possession. We belong to Him. "We are His people, and the sheep of His pasture" (Psalm 100:3).

What, then, will He do, if we fail to obey Him? The writer of the Epistle to the Hebrews answers our question. "Whom the Lord loveth He chasteneth, and scourgeth every son whom He receiveth" (Hebrews 12:6). If we give no attention to our Lord's gentle persuasion, we may be compelled to "lie down" as the result of His firm rebuke. But even the severest chastening is not without His love. The trials of life are not to punish us, but to correct us, that we might appreciate and appropriate all God has provided.

All of us are guilty of the same error. We foolishly neglect fellowship with the Lord and feel that we can do things *for* Him without taking time to be *with* Him. Jeremiah confessed his own inability to accomplish anything in himself saying, "O LORD, I know that the way of man is not in himself: it is not in man that walketh to direct his steps" (Jeremiah 10:23). We need to remind ourselves of this fact constantly. We forget so easily. It is when we forget that God must do something about it. For it is absolutely certain that the child of God, who refuses or neglects to follow the leading and direction of the Great Shepherd, cannot know real happiness. He may think he is happy, but he is missing God's best. Lasting happiness is contingent on doing the will of God. For only God knows the future.

Why are the shepherds in Palestine so concerned that their sheep follow the shepherd to the pasture? Why not allow the sheep to wander and graze at will? In Palestine pasture land is very scarce. The absence of fences and the scarcity of pasture make it necessary that every sheep belong to a flock and that every flock have its shepherd. It is the shepherd's responsibility, not that of the sheep, to find good pasture. The sheep must depend entirely on the wisdom of the shepherd to guide them.

In Ezekiel 34:14 the Lord says of His sheep, "I will feed them in a good pasture . . . and in a fat pasture shall they feed." God knows where the "good pasture" can be found. We need to rely upon Him to lead us. Submission to His guidance can avert the calamities and escape the tragedies. Only His divine foresight can choose the best.

Child of God, you may be suffering under the arm of God's discipline at this moment. I am not saying all suffering is the result of our failure to obey the revealed will of God. Yet, much of it is. Could it be that you are a believer in the Lord Jesus Christ, but even though He is your Great Shepherd, you have been seeking out your own pasture? You have been neglecting to spend time in the presence of the Lord, fellowshipping with Him, and feeding upon His blessed Word. Your soul is starving. As a result, you are a defeated, miserable, and unhappy Christian. Confess to God! Get right with Him! May it not be necessary for Him to make you "lie down in the green pastures." Submit! Yield all to Him! Lie down at His feet willingly, then, like rested, well-fed sheep you will know contentment. You will be satisfied with Christ.

5.

THE PEACE

"He leadeth me beside the still waters"

So often amidst the hurry and scurry of life the believer in Christ finds himself being swept along in the busy rush of the world. Quiet time being neglected, he fails to rest in the presence of God. Sometimes our Great Shepherd, the Lord Jesus, must force us to take the necessary respite and pause. "He *maketh* me to lie down in green pastures." Rarely does He impel us to do things, but occasionally He must. Rather than compulsion, His much-used principle seems to be attraction. "He *leadeth* me beside the still waters."

Throughout the Scriptures we read repeatedly of our Lord's faithfulness in leading His own in the way of blessing. Like us, they did not always follow. But nevertheless, God showered His love upon them and continued to watch over them. David writes in Psalm 139: 7-10, "Whither shall I go from Thy Spirit? or whither shall I flee from Thy presence? If I ascend up into heaven, Thou art there: if I make my bed in hell, behold, Thou art there. If I take the wings of the morning, and dwell in the uttermost parts of the sea; *Even there shall*

Thy hand lead me, and Thy right hand shall hold me."
The Lord always precedes His own throughout every
experience of life. Whether it be joy or sorrow, health
or sickness, prosperity or depression, He is there to guide
and direct.

Even more astonishing is the fact that the best is yet
to come. The Lord Jesus promises believers that after
this life is over and they are safely in His visible presence, He will continue to lead. "For the Lamb which is
in the midst of the throne shall feed them, *and shall lead
them* unto living fountains of waters: and God shall
wipe away all tears from their eyes" (Revelation 7:17).
It has been a joyous privilege to know the Lord and to
feel His nearness as He has led through the strange paths
of life. But oh, the glorious confidence He has given that
there is an eternity of blessing to come when His followers shall see Him face to face.

With a heart overflowing with praise David says in
the Twenty-third Psalm, "He leadeth me beside the still
waters." The "still waters" suggest to me God's comforting and sustaining peace. David used the expression
from his own experience as a shepherd. He had to lead
his dry and thirsty sheep to a water brook or cistern
for much needed water. He well knew, as does any
shepherd, that even though the sheep may be extremely
thirsty, they will not drink from gurgling water. Turbid
or ruffled streams frighten the sheep. They will only
drink from "still waters," surrounded by quietness and
tranquillity. Thus, it is not only the shepherd's respon-

sibility to lead his sheep to water, but he must provide the perfect peace they require to slack their thirst.

This is precisely what the Great Shepherd has done for His sheep. He was born into a world of sin that knew nothing of the waters of peace. There was plenty of water, but turbulent and disturbing, unable to quench the spiritual thirst of sinful hearts. For centuries helpless and condemned souls vainly sought to provide their own waters, degenerating into further hopelessness. God says in Jeremiah 2:13, "For My people have committed two evils; they have forsaken Me the fountain of living waters, and hewed them out cisterns, broken cisterns, that can hold no water." This pathetic condition still exists. Spiritually thirsty, their souls famished, many continue in their search for the satisfying water of life. Neglecting to come to Christ, they know nothing of the "still waters" of God's goodness and grace. We live in an age of nervousness, depression, frustration, and fear because unbelieving men and women are content to drink from the "broken cisterns that can hold no water."

Americans take about three billion sleeping pills a year plus millions of other drugs. Many are gradually becoming addicted to the so-called "tranquillizing" drugs. Be sure, peace can never be found in pills or drugs. Peace is found "beside the still waters." We discover the "still waters" through Him who said, "If any man thirst, let him come unto Me, and drink" (John 7:37). "Whosoever drinketh of the water that I shall give him shall never thirst; but the water that I shall give him shall be in him a well of water springing up unto everlasting life" (John 4:14). Here is the satisfying water of the living Christ. Those who drink of this water will "never thirst." They will know the peace of God that forever banishes restlessness and fear.

It was not always easy for the Oriental shepherd to find an adequate watering place for his sheep. Nor was it easy for our Lord to provide the "still waters." He had to suffer and die on the cross to prepare the way. Prompted by His great love for His sheep, He willingly made the sacrifice. Because of the price He paid, we now may come and drink of the "still waters."

There are so many troubled minds and hearts in the world today because they have not believed on the Lord Jesus Christ. Oh, that they might realize that the moment they believe on Him, they become the eternal possessors of His peace. We read in Romans 5:1, "Therefore being justified by faith, we have peace with God through our Lord Jesus Christ." What a wealth of blessedness in these words, "we have peace with God." His wonderful peace is immediately possessed by all who sincerely trust in Him. Here is peace unaffected by circumstances, unchanged by time, underlying all life's experiences, however ruffled the surface may be. "Peace with God, through our Lord Jesus Christ," is yours for believing.

The Lord Jesus said in John 14:27, "Peace I leave with you, My peace I give unto you: not as the world giveth, give I unto you." The world makes an offer of peace, but it is unreal. The world can only give temporary peace. Christ gives eternal peace. The world gives peace as a doctor gives an anesthetic. Christ gives peace that is life, hope, and strength. The peace the world gives is merely on the surface. Christ gives heart peace. Actually, the world doesn't even *give* peace. It sells it. It demands lust, fleshly indulgence, and painful sinfulness in payment. The peace which Christ offers is bestowed as a free gift. "My peace I *give* unto you." The world's peace operates only in peaceful and favorable circumstances. Christ gives peace which is effectual under any circumstances.

If millions throughout the world would turn to Christ and drink from the "still waters" of His peace, their trouble and misery would disappear immediately. Only in Christ do we find the strength and grace to face the trials of life peacefully. Without the Lord Jesus we have knowledge, but not wisdom; houses, but not homes; speed, but not direction; medicine, but not health. It is Christ who really makes life worth living.

One of the greatest enemies of our day which brings sadness to thousands of homes is mental illness. Amidst the ever-accelerating tempo of modern life, because of the terrifying uncertainties of the future and the tragic drift toward extreme sinfulness, the minds of both old and young are being broken. One governmental agency says that five people in every hundred need some type of psychiatric care at some period during their lifetime.

Another source, the National Mental Health Foundation, estimates that this figure should be as high as 10 per cent. Is there no solution for this pathetic loss of mental balance and health? Ah yes, "the peace of God." Believe on Christ. Follow Him to the "still waters" and you will find peace and rest for your soul.

The Bible speaks about "peace with God" and the "peace of God." "Peace with God" has to do with our relationship with Christ. The "peace of God" concerns our fellowship with Him. We do not make "peace with God." All we need do is to receive it. Christ provided "peace with God" when He died on the cross and rose again for our sins. Believing on Him, we have "peace with God." As long as we do God's will and daily confess all known sin to Him, we enjoy His fellowship in the "peace of God." To persist in sin, failing to forsake it and to confess it, severs our fellowship with Him. The "peace with God" remains but not the "peace of God."

Let me illustrate. Suppose I enter a home where there are three small sons. Two of them are in the living room with their parents, but the third is upstairs because of disobedience. The wayward child has not broken his family relationship. He is still just as much a member of the family as ever. What has he done? He has broken fellowship with his loved ones. Until he says he is sorry and promises to do better, he remains separated from the family circle. So it is in Christ. When one believes, he enters into an eternal relationship with Christ which can never be broken. He becomes a member of God's family. But by disobedience, he may break fellowship with the Lord and lose the "peace of God." If there is repentance and confession to God, the believer is forgiven and fellowship is restored.

For the believer who is living in daily fellowship with the Lord, the assuring promises of Philippians 4:6, 7, are always a present reality. "Do not be overanxious about anything, but by prayer and earnest pleading, together with thanksgiving, let your requests be unreservedly made known in the presence of God. And then the *peace of God*, which transcends all our powers of thought, will be a garrison to guard your hearts and minds in union with Christ" (Weymouth's translation). The peace God speaks about here is not something worked up, but poured in. It is supernatural. Coming from God, it completely compensates for all our human limitations. No one can fully comprehend it. Indeed, it is far beyond intellectual analysis. We cannot describe its processes. But we can certainly testify to its fact. It is real!

One reason why it is so real is that it is given by Him who perfectly understands every situation of life. The Lord Jesus never learns about our troubles. He knows about them. Christians do not suffer alone. God suffers with them. He always goes before. "He leadeth me." What we suffer, must first of all be endured by Him. A wise shepherd never permits his sheep to drink until he first tests the water himself. Our Great Shepherd has done the same. He "was in all points tempted like as we are, yet without sin" (Hebrews 4:15). He did not resist nor seek to escape. As a faithful Shepherd He drank of the poisoned waters "that He by the grace of God should taste death for every man" (Hebrews 2:9). He died that we might be eternally delivered from the penalty and power of sin.

Are you going through a time in your life when it seems hopeless and useless to continue? Don't give up. Rest in the Lord. Drink of the "still waters." Christ understands. He knows what it is to be lonely and forsaken. Friends and even dearest loved ones turned their faces from Him in the darkest hour of His life. He knows all about poverty, pain, and disappointment. He realizes what it is to drink of the bitter cup of woe and sorrow. He understands. To all the weary and forlorn he says, "Come unto Me, all ye that labour and are heavy laden, and I will give you rest" (Matthew 11:28). There is peaceful rest "beside the still waters" for all who will come to Christ and follow Him.

6.

THE PRIVILEGE

"He restoreth my soul"

In supplying the wants and needs of his sheep, the shepherd leads them to the "green pastures" for rich, nourishing food and rejuvenating rest. Next he locates a brook or cistern with quiet and peaceful surroundings where the sheep may enjoy refreshing drink without fear. Having eaten, rested, and drunk, the sheep are now ready to journey homeward.

With such abundant provisions, it might be thought that the helpless sheep would never leave the watchful care of their shepherd. But occasionally they did. Most of the roads and paths on which they traveled were extremely narrow. The fields of grain on either side often proved to be too great a temptation. One little nibble, and then another, until deeper and deeper the sheep went into the field, satisfying his hunger. Soon he was completely lost from the rest of the flock. Worst of all, he was lost from the shepherd's care. Usually it was not long until the shepherd missed his sheep and hastily darted back, looking and searching for him. How happy he was when he finally found the disobedient wanderer.

Then, with his usual affection he "restored" the lost sheep to the flock.

When David said of his Lord, "He restoreth my soul," doubtless his thinking was reflecting back to the years of his youth when he, too, as a shepherd, had sought out helpless sheep and restored them to the fold. Such retrospecting may also have prompted memories of his own failure in wandering from the Lord as he shamefully yielded to the lusts of his flesh. For an entire year David was completely separated from the joy of fellowship with the Lord. Never had he been so miserable and unhappy in all his life. But, praise God, he did not remain in that condition. He repented and came back. The Fifty-first Psalm tells the story. Hear his pathetic cry from a heart broken by the bitterness of sin. "Restore unto me the joy of Thy salvation" (Psalm 51:12). As He always does, God answered this earnest prayer. Restoration followed. Later David compared the joy of fellowship with God with the emptiness of the superficial and sinful pleasures of the world. Without question real joy could only be found in fellowship with God. With a heart overflowing in gratitude he voiced praise to the Lord, "Thou wilt shew me the path of life: in Thy presence is fulness of joy; at Thy right hand there are pleasures for evermore" (Psalm 16:11). David learned the hard way, but once and for all he discovered that real happiness is found only in fellowship with God.

All believers are like David in the respect that there

are times when we, too, wander from our Lord's marvelous provision and care. Our hearts grow cold. We lose our vision of the work that needs to be done. With little concern for the gospel and lost souls, we live for ourselves. Lethargy and indifference snuff out the flame of passion that once burned within us. We lose our "first love" and with it, the joy of our salvation. It is so easy to lose our spiritual fervor for Christ. We may be fiery hot for Him today, but lukewarm or icy cold tomorrow. The hymn writer expressed our waywardness well when he wrote: "Prone to wander, Lord, I feel it, Prone to leave the Lord I love."

Considering our Great Shepherd's limitless provision of the "Bread of Life," the "Living Waters," and the "perfect peace," we might well wonder how anyone could forsake all this for the pleasures of sin. But we all do. Satan makes sin so appealing and alluring. Not until after we have submitted to his shallow and deceitful claims do we find them to be ridiculous and foolish.

Satan lures us in many ways, but one of his well-worn methods is to try to keep Christians comfortable. "Seek your own comfort," he whispers in our ears, "and all will be well." Regrettably, we listen and believe him. We build bigger houses and cram them with all the latest gadgets. We accumulate and store up treasure for ourselves. Caught in the thinking of the worldly-minded, we feel that security and happiness are found in "things." The Lord Jesus taught just the opposite in

Luke 12:15, "Beware of covetousness: for a man's life consisteth not in the abundance of *things* which he possesseth." Let us not be deceived, "things" cannot produce happiness and ineffable joy. Christ does! He was born into the world to bring "good tidings of great joy" (Luke 2:10). Everyone who believes on Him receives this "great joy" as a gift. There is a danger, however, that we may stray from the Lord and lose, not our salvation, but the *joy* of our salvation. This is not God's will for any of us. He says in John 15:11, "These things have I spoken unto you, that My joy might *remain* in you, and that your joy might be *full*." From this passage it is obvious that the Lord desires that we revel in His joy every day of our lives.

How can we best guard against loss of the marvelous gift of God's wonderful joy? By spending time communing with Him. No matter how mature we may be as Christians, none of us is strong enough to face the tempter alone. "Wherefore let him that thinketh he standeth take heed lest he fall" (1 Corinthians 10:12). "Our help is in the name of the LORD, who made heaven and earth" (Psalm 124:8). We are weak and needy, but the Lord is strong and all-sufficient. If we are to enjoy His strength, it is obligatory that we carefully set apart a definite time each day, preferably the first thing in the morning, to commune and fellowship with God in prayer.

It is interesting to note that even each sheep had a time of quietness and aloneness with his shepherd every

day. Early in the morning the sheep would form a grazing line and keep the same position throughout the day.
At some time along the way each sheep left the grazing
line and went to the shepherd. The shepherd received
the sheep with outstretched arms speaking kindly to it.
The sheep would rub against the shepherd's leg, or if
the shepherd were seated, rub its cheek against his face.
Meanwhile the shepherd would gently pat the sheep,
rubbing its nose and ears and scratching its chin. After
a brief period of this intimate fellowship together, the
sheep returned to its place in the grazing line.

If even the sheep have the need of "communing"
with their shepherd each day, how much more important
it is for those of us who claim to love Christ to recognize
the importance of spending time with Him. If we are
truly to follow the Lord Jesus, we must be men and
women of prayer.

Have you ever noticed in your Bible reading how
faithful the Lord Jesus was in communing with the
Father? Though burdened with the busy ministry of
healing the multitudes, He realized the necessity of with-
drawing for prayer. "Great multitudes came together to
hear, and to be healed by Him of their infirmities. And
He withdrew Himself into the wilderness, and prayed"
(Luke 5:15-16). In Mark 1:35 we read that "in the morning, rising up a great while before day, he went out,
and departed into a solitary place, and there prayed."
On another occasion He "went out into a mountain to
pray, and continued all night in prayer to God" (Luke

6:12). When Peter was about to be tested Jesus said to him, "Simon, Simon, behold, Satan hath desired to have you, that he may sift you as wheat: But I have prayed for thee, that thy faith fail not" (Luke 22:31-32). In John 14:16 He tells the disciples that He would pray to the Father for the coming of another Comforter, the Holy Spirit. Who can read the intercessory prayer of our Lord in John 17 without sensing His tireless concern for prayer? He prayed as He hung from the cross, "Father, forgive them; for they know not what they do" (Luke 23:34). Just before He died He prayed, "Father, into Thy hands I commend My spirit" (Luke 23:46). As our risen and ascended Saviour He still prays at the right hand of the Father. "He ever liveth to make intercession" (Hebrews 7:25).

If the Lord Jesus, who was sinless, gave Himself so unreservedly to the practice of prayer, how can we—poor, weak, dependent creatures—live without it? To all Christians our Lord says, "Enter into thy closet, and when thou hast shut thy door, pray to thy Father which is in secret; and thy Father which seeth in secret shall reward thee openly" (Matthew 6:6). Let nothing interfere with your quiet time with God. If there is anything preventing this necessary fellowship with Christ, forsake it and get rid of it immediately.

A businessman told his pastor he was so busy he didn't have time to pray. The wise pastor replied, "If you have so much business to attend to that you have no time to pray, then you have more business on hand than God ever intended you to have." How true. Anything that hinders prayer in the believer's life does not belong in the life.

Failure to commune with God will make us easy marks for temptation and sin. When we are out of touch with God anything can happen. The bars will be lowered. Sin will find its way into our hearts. Spiritual things will become less and less interesting. Worldliness will be most appealing. From this state it is quite easy to drift into indifference completely oblivious to the claim of Christ. Of course with the loss of interest in Him, the radiant joy we once had completely disappears.

Suppose one has drifted into this backslidden state. Suppose the light of Christ in the heart has been clouded by sin. What can be done? The same thing David did: confess the sin to the Lord and repent. Then with new-found joy you will say as did David, "He restoreth my soul."

Are you out of fellowship with God? He desires that you come back. He will receive you. This is your *privilege* as a Christian. God knew how unstable and changeable we would be. He foresaw our weaknesses and provided in advance. In 1 John 2:1-2 we read, "My little children, these things write I unto you, that ye sin not. And if any man sin, we have an advocate with the Father, Jesus Christ the righteous: And He is the propitiation for our sins." The Lord was crucified not only for some of our sins, but for all: past, present, and future. Because of His completed sacrifice, immediate forgiveness and restoration is available to all believers. John further tells us that, "If we confess our sins, He [God] is faithful and just to forgive us our sins, and to cleanse us from all unrighteousness" (1 John 1:9). God will never refuse to forgive the repentant believer. He promises immediate forgiveness if we confess to Him. We are not to beg for forgiveness, but receive it on the grounds of Christ's sacrifice. At the very instant He forgives us He restores us into fellowship and communion with Him.

Could it be that you have wandered away from the love and mercy of your Great Shepherd? You are a Christian but like a wandering sheep you have strayed into strange paths. In all probability it began when you neglected prayer or possibly you chose the wrong companions. Or was it the practice of a secret sin that drew you away from Christ? It matters little which. The fact remains, if you will come back to God, He will forgive you and restore your soul.

There is always the tendency after sinning against the Lord to run from Him and hide as did Adam and Eve. In love, God came looking for them, calling, "Where art thou?" How foolish they were. It was bad enough to sin and sever precious fellowship with the Lord, but to try to hide from Him was even worse, especially when we realize it was not an angry God searching for Adam with a club, but a God of mercy ready and willing to forgive.

But our present problem is not, "Where is Adam?"

but "Where art thou?" Are you in fellowship with Christ or is it true of you as Isaiah declares, "Your iniquities have separated between you and your God, and your sins have hid His face from you, that He will not hear" (Isaiah 59:2)? If you confess, He will hear and forgive.

Child of God, away from the Lord, come back to Him, will you? You know you cannot have real joy out of fellowship with Christ. The seat of blessing is in the center of the will of God. Confess your sin to Him and He will "restore" your soul.

7.

THE PATHWAY

*"He leadeth me in the paths of righteousness
for His name's sake"*

The Great Shepherd, the Lord Jesus Christ, is ever before His own, leading all along the way. There are times, however, when because of the old nature, we yield to the weakness of the flesh and fail to follow. What does the Shepherd do? He seeks us out, and if we confess our sin, He "restores" us, placing us back into fellowship with Himself. Does He put us on probation to see if we can hold out? Indeed He does not! He treats us just the same as He did before, leading us in His divinely chosen *pathway*. David says, "He leadeth me in the paths of righteousness for His name's sake." Literally the "paths of righteousness" are the "right paths." God knows how weak and helpless we are. We have proved this to Him and to ourselves time and time again by our own waywardness. Thus He promises that if we simply follow, He will choose the "right paths" for us.

How foolish we are to think we can accomplish anything in life without His perfect guidance. Sheep do not know what awaits them on the path ahead, but the shepherd does. He knows the best paths to choose. It is for this reason we need to depend upon our Great Shepherd for everything.

Even in the days of the prosperous Roman rule there were few good roads in Palestine. Most of them were winding footpaths, about twenty inches wide. Confused travelers often lost their way because of the uncertainty of these paths. Some ended abruptly in a field, others led to a waterway or a dangerous cliff. Obviously it was well-nigh impossible for sheep to go anywhere without the shepherd. You and I are no different. It is one thing to believe on Christ. It is quite another thing to let Him plan the life and lead along His way.

A common tragedy is to see one believe on the Lord Jesus and start out well in his Christian experience only to end up a total disgrace as far as the will of God is concerned. To know God's will is man's greatest treasure; to do His will is man's greatest privilege. To know God's will we must have no ends of our own to serve. We must be completely yielded to the Lord Jesus, ready and willing to follow wherever He leads. Those living in this place of humble submission to Him will always hear the unfailing voice from behind saying, "This is the way, walk ye in it" (Isaiah 30:21).

We do not like to admit it, but is it not true, that by the very manner in which most of us live, we feel we are able to do much better for ourselves than Christ can? Rather than wait on Him, we surge ahead, conniving schemes and pulling strings trying to effect our own selfish plans, rather than seek His leading and direction. We feel we are unable to wait. With pious words we say, "God's work must be done *now*." But remember God's work can only be done in God's time and in God's way. Christian service performed in this manner will never lack for His blessing.

There are scores of illustrations of this in the Scriptures. Take Kadesh-barnea for example. Two years after the children of Israel were delivered from their Egyptian bondage, they sent out spies from Kadesh-barnea to search out the Promised Land. Later, upon hearing the report of the spies they became fearful and refused to follow God's plan. They thought they could do the job a better way. What was the result? Thirty-eight years in the wilderness! Finally, after all their wandering they came to Kadesh-barnea again. This time they obeyed God and by faith entered the Promised Land. But think of the wasted years. Thirty-eight years is more than half the life span of the average human.

Let us not be too critical of the children of Israel. All of us have Kadesh-barneas in our lives. Again and again because of haste and lack of faith we have been forced to return to the starting point and begin all over. Too often life is spent going around in circles rather than upward and forward, gaining the spiritual heights and advancement the Lord has chosen for us. More than anything else in the world we need to be in the center of God's will, "the paths of righteousness." In Ephesians

5:17 the apostle writes, "Wherefore be ye not unwise, but understanding what the will of the Lord is." Seek God's will and do it and you can never go wrong. If you are not sure of God's will for your life, wait. Don't make a move until you are certain. In His own time the Lord will make His mind clear to the undecided heart. You cannot go wrong by waiting. But you may make a tragic mistake by rushing.

Moses was a perfect example of one who waited for the will of God. He went up into the Mount to be alone with the Lord for forty days and forty nights and was given a pattern. He came down from the Mount with his pattern and built the Tabernacle in God's way, according to God's specifications. There was no waste of time, materials, energy, or personnel. The secret of the success lay in the fact that Moses waited on the Lord before he acted.

Samuel Brengle, one of the great saints of the Salvation Army, once said, "If I were dying and had the privilege of delivering a last exhortation to all the Christians of the world, and that message had to be condensed into three words, I would say, 'Wait on God.'"

It is very possible that you want the will of God for your life, but you are confused as to how to find it. How may one determine the Lord's will for his life? I would say the foremost requisite is a willingness in the heart to obey. If you desire to know God's will for speculative purposes or for thinking it over, you will never know it. There must be a distinct and earnest desire to follow the Lord in the paths He chooses. God places no requisite before obedience. He says, "To obey is better than sacrifice" (1 Samuel 15:22).

All of us could learn a lesson from the Scotch shepherd dog. If left to guard his master's coat, he will not leave it until the master returns. Nothing can draw him from the task to which he is appointed. Even though a rabbit may hop almost under his nose, the obedient dog will not move. A deer might dart across the glen so close that the dog could easily catch it, but he does not budge. I suppose if the dog had a mind like some Christians, he might reason, "Certainly my master was unaware that a rabbit would pass or a very valuable deer. Surely he expects me to run after them." But no, the Scotch shepherd dog is faithful to his assigned task.

Those who are ready and willing to obey God's will are in a position to seek His leading. How may this be determined? There are three ways by which God speaks to us: Bible reading, prayer, and circumstances.

I have never known the Lord to lead anyone contrary to that which is written in the Scriptures. It would be ridiculous for God to give us a Book to live by and then direct us to do just the opposite. God speaks through His Word. The faithful diligent study of the Bible often provides the light to guide us along "the paths of righteousness." James writes, "If any of you lack wisdom, let him ask of God . . . and it shall be given him"(James 1:5). Frequently this divine wisdom is found through the regular reading of the Bible.

God also speaks to us as we pray. Prayer can be communion. Communion is two-sided. Not only do we speak in prayer, we patiently listen. We should converse with God. But we should also give Him an opportunity to speak. Usually He is more willing to speak than impatient believers are to listen. Real praying is not a hasty five-minute session in the morning or a sleepy sentence or two in the evening. We are to "pray without ceasing," waiting on God.

We also determine the Lord's will through providential circumstances. We may be guided through a word spoken by a friend or loved one, or by something said in a sermon, or by a line or two we might read in a book, or through the promptings of the indwelling Holy Spirit.

Thus, as we wait on God through Bible reading, prayer, and circumstances, we shall discover the mind of God. All three will be in harmony. One is not sufficient in itself for divine guidance. Someone has said, "Bible study alone, without prayer, will produce a Pharisee. Prayer alone, without a knowledge of God's word will produce a fanatic. Using circumstances alone for guidance, without the Bible and prayer, will produce a fatalist." All three working in perfect unity will enable us to discern the Lord's leading.

Of course, after we have determined God's will, we must do it. Jesus said, "If ye know these things, happy are ye if ye do them" (John 13:17). Happiness is not found merely in a knowledge of the will of God, but in the doing of it. Many a life has drifted off into failure by refusing to do what God wanted.

The greatest mistake in life is to say "No" to God. On occasion I have had older people tell me how, at one time, they experienced a definite leading that God wanted them to go into the ministry or to be a missionary. They refused to heed the call. They were most regretful that they failed to obey God. Some have even told of a life of misery and grief as the result of their disobedience.

A pastor relates a similar experience of a young Christian school teacher who came to his study in tears. Amidst sobs she said, "For two years I have felt that I should seek preparation for missionary work in India. But when I mentioned it to mother she scolded me, and told me I must never speak of such a thing again."

"What can I say," asked the pastor, "when your mother objects? But," he continued, "if God wants you in India, I think you had better go."

Then she took thirty dollars from her purse and said, "I know I cannot go, but I want to send this to India to employ a native worker."

The pastor took the money saying, "Do as you wish; but realize, if God wants you in India, thirty dollars does not buy off your call."

She went away weeping. Six months later she married a grocery clerk, who, shortly after, broke her heart. Seven years later the pastor was called back from another city to officiate at the girl's funeral. As he stood by the casket and saw the heartbroken mother sitting near, he could not help recalling what happened eight years before, saying to himself, "O mother, why did you not let God have His way with your daughter?"

How different it was in the home of Dr. John T. Gracey. When he was a boy in Sunday school, he surrendered his life to Christ. Returning home, he went to his father and told him what he had done and that he thought God wanted him to be a missionary. The father replied, "My son, go and do your duty even though you die for it."

Then John told his mother. She said, "I would rather die without a crust than have you disobey the call of God." John T. Gracey's name will go down in history as one of the greatest missionaries of his church.

There is no place of greater blessing or happiness than the center of God's will. Abraham's servant said, "I being in the way, the Lord led me" (Genesis 24:27). Here is the secret of real joy. God makes no mistakes when He leads us. He leads "for His name's sake." He cannot possibly fail His mighty Name.

Have you entrusted your life to Him? Are you wholly following Him? If not, seek His will, then permit Him to guide you in the "right paths" for His great "name's sake."

8.

THE PRESENCE

*"Yea, though I walk through the valley
of the shadow of death, I will fear no
evil for thou art with me"*

Divinely-chosen paths are always best for the child of God. There is no place of greater security or safety than following the Great Shepherd in the way of His choice. Thus with unwavering faith David could say, "He leadeth me in the paths of righteousness for His name's sake."

It is not always easy, however, to follow the Lord. Sometimes the "paths of righteousness" wind "through the valley of the shadow of death." But those who truly follow Christ can say as did David, "I will fear no evil: for Thou art with me." It matters not where the Great Shepherd leads. All will be well. We have the unquestionable promise of His *presence.* What more do we need? "Our sufficiency is of God" (2 Corinthians 3:5). Because of the reality of His nearness we are assured of His "all sufficiency in all things" enabling us to "abound to every good work" (2 Corinthians 9:8).

In our foregoing studies we have watched the Shepherd tenderly caring for His sheep, leading them to the "green pastures," and then to the "still waters." Wanderers from the flock were restored. Now He leads them over the "right paths," toward home. There were times when it was necessary to go through the dreaded "valley of the shadow of death."

Actually there is such a valley in Palestine. One writer in describing this valley says, "Every sheepherder from Spain to Dalmatia knows of it. It is south of the Jericho Road leading from Jerusalem to the Dead Sea and is a narrow defile through a mountain range. Climatic and grazing conditions make it necessary for the sheep to be moved through this valley for seasonal feeding each year.

"The valley is four and a half miles long. Its side walls are over 1500 feet high in places and it is only ten or twelve feet wide at the bottom. Travel through the valley is dangerous, because its floor, badly eroded by cloudbursts, has gullies seven or eight feet deep. Actual footing on solid rock is so narrow in many places that a sheep cannot turn around, and it is an unwritten law of shepherds that flocks must go up the valley in the morning hours and down toward the eventide, lest flocks meet in the defile.

"About halfway through the valley the walk crosses from one side to the other at a place where the path is cut in two by an eight-foot gully. One section of the path is about eighteen inches higher than the other; the sheep must jump across it. The shepherd stands at this break and coaxes or forces the sheep to make the leap. If a sheep slips and lands in the gully, the shepherd's crook is encircled around a large sheep's neck or a small sheep's chest, and it is lifted to safety.

"Many wild dogs lurk in the shadows of the valley looking for prey. After a band of sheep has entered the defile, the leading sheep may come upon such a dog. Unable to retreat, the leader 'baas' a warning. The shepherd, skilled in throwing his rod, hurls it at the dog and knocks the animal into the washed-out gully where it is easily killed. Thus the sheep have learned to fear no evil in the Valley of the Shadow of Death, for their master is there to aid them and protect them from harm."

To be sure, no follower of the Great Shepherd, the Lord Jesus Christ, can expect to avoid the "valley of the shadow of death." The "paths of righteousness" lead through this "valley."

But may I ask, "What is the valley of the shadow of death about which David speaks?" Though this verse has been quoted by saints in every age for comfort and assurance at death, it would seem from verse five that David was not thinking primarily of death. For indeed there are no enemies "in the presence" of the believer after he dies. He enters the visible presence of the Lord immediately to "dwell in the house of the LORD for ever." Paul said, while speaking of death, that he had "a desire to depart, and to be with Christ" (Philippians 1:23). He was conscious of the great truth that when the believer closes his eyes in physical death, at that instant the soul is translated into the glorious presence of the Lord Jesus.

I believe that the "valley of the shadow of death" refers to the many trials of life believers must face. Sorrow and suffering of all kinds are a part of "the valley" experience. It could refer as well to the agony often experienced before death or the sorrow that frequently shrouds loved ones after death, but never death itself. Christ in His death and resurrection removed the darkness from death. So for the true believer in Christ, death is the gate of entry into the presence of our Lord.

Until our Great Shepherd calls us to abide in the "house of the Lord forever," we must follow Him even though the strange paths may lead us into sickness, sorrow, or suffering. The Bible does not promise freedom from discomfort or anguish in this life. Rather we see just the opposite as Job writes, "Man is born unto trouble" (Job 5:7), a consequence of Adam and Eve's sin (Genesis 3:16-19). Trials are to be expected. Christians are by no means immune. The way of the cross is not a path of ease and comfort; oftentimes we are led through deep sorrow and great trials. Indeed the Lord told His disciples, "In the world ye shall have tribulation." But they were not to despair. "These things have I spoken unto you, that in Me ye might have peace . . . be of good cheer; I have overcome the world" (John 16:33).

Praise God, the true believer is never alone. He walks by divine appointment, the eye of the Lord is upon him, the hand of the Lord sustains him. Christ feels the pain of every aching nerve in the body. He senses the stress of the disturbed mind. He understands the grief of the breaking heart. Indeed, Christ knows of all the uncertainties and testings of the "valley." "Thou art with me," David declares. Christ is always with His own. Never does He leave them. "Lo, I am with you alway, even unto the end of the world" (Matthew 28:20). For this reason David could say "I will fear no evil."

Sometimes God's people do fear evil. Oh, what misery fear has brought into the lives of so many Christians. We say we are not afraid. We should not be, but we are. Most of us are like the little fellow who came dashing up the cellar stairs into the kitchen, where his two older brothers were washing and drying the dishes.

"Are you afraid?" one of them asked with a laugh.

"Oh no," he replied. "I'm not afraid. For Jesus goes with me. But I have to hurry away from the black shadows."

It is not necessary for the true believer to fear even the shadows. A dog can bite, but his shadow cannot harm us. A wicked man may destroy us, but his shadow cannot. A shadow is the counterpart of its substance. In itself it cannot harm us. David declares, we "walk through the valley of the shadow of death." Not the valley of death, but only the "shadow."

Even in the shadows of sorrow, anxiety, death, or whatever it may be, we are not alone. For every shadow is produced by a light. The stronger the shadow, the brighter the light. It is impossible to have a shadow without a light. The Lord Jesus said, "I am the light of the world: he that followeth Me shall not walk in darkness, but shall have the light of life" (John 8:12). Our Lord reveals in this verse that the believer "shall not walk in darkness." This means he shall not *continue* in darkness. There may be darkness along the way. In fact, the "valley of the shadow of death" is more literally translated "the valley of deep darkness." When the shepherd took his sheep into the valley, it was not to stay, but to pass through. Our Great Shepherd does the same. He leads us into the valley, but never to remain in it. Always while passing through we have the Light. Christ is there. We "shall have the light of life." It is His glorious *presence* that comforts and sustains. The believer can well understand what David meant when he said, "Thou art with me."

How foolish for the child of God to fear anything. Yet how often we are disturbed about the future. We dread that the unexpected will happen. We fear the secret working of some enemy, the possibility of poverty, the uncertainty of employment, the loss of loved ones, and a host of other things. Yet over eighty times in His Word, God says, "fear not." Hear His voice, "Fear thou not; for I am with thee; be not dismayed; for I am thy God: I will strengthen thee; yea, I will help thee; yea, I will uphold thee with the right hand of My righteousness" (Isaiah 41:10).

Doubtless the child of God is fearful because of an unsurrendered heart. God tells us in 1 John 4:18, "There is no fear in love; but perfect love casteth out fear: because fear hath torment. He that feareth is not made perfect in love." How do we get rid of the plague of fear? Love Christ more. Surrender your life fully to Him. Commit everything to His keeping. Then you will worry about nothing. Love Him fully and fear will be routed out.

In Proverbs 9:10 we are told that "the fear of the Lord is the beginning of wisdom." Our only fear should be that of fearing God. This does not mean to be afraid of Him, but reverently to trust Him for all things with a holy hatred for evil. When Adam said, "I was afraid" (Genesis 3:10), this was not the "fear" that is "the beginning of wisdom." He was frightened because of his disobedience. This was the "fright" of the Lord rather than the "fear" of the Lord.

Since Christ is with us, we have nothing to fear. Every need will be provided. "The Lord is my Shepherd; I shall not want." I shall not want for *rest*, "He maketh me to lie down in green pastures." I shall not want for *refreshment*, "He leadeth me beside the still waters." I shall not want for *forgiveness*, "He restoreth my soul." I shall not want for *guidance*, "He leadeth me in the paths of righteousness for His name's sake." I shall not

want for *anything*, "for Thou art with me." What need
have I, since my Great Shepherd leads me on step by
step, even though it may be through the "valley of deep
darkness"?

I really believe the Lord takes us through the "valley
of deep darkness" occasionally, to remind us of His
nearness. We are so forgetful of the Lord's mercies
that we need an occasional reminder.

You will note that it is at this point in the Psalm
that David seems to get closer to the Lord than ever.
Up to this verse he has been speaking in the third
person and using the personal pronoun "He." "*He*
leadeth." "*He* maketh." "*He* restoreth." When David
comes to speak of the "valley of the deep darkness,"
the third personal pronoun is changed to the second:
"Yea, though I walk through the valley of the shadow
of death, I will fear no evil; for *Thou* art with me." We
can easily sense the fact of David's drawing closer to
his Great Shepherd as he passes through the precipitous
and treacherous paths of the dark valley. Most valley
experiences have this effect on us. Examining our hearts
and acknowledging our sins, we get closer to the Lord.
Our trials seem to move us to say anew, "That I may
know Him, and the power of His resurrection, and the
fellowship of His sufferings, being made conformable
unto His death" (Philippians 3:10).

A father told me one time, "I never really knew the
Lord until He took my little boy home to be with
Himself." Many of us have had similar experiences. We

frequently discover our Shepherd's great love in the dark valleys.

The Lord may be leading you through a dark valley at this moment. But if you know Christ, be assured, you will not stay in the valley. Believe Him. Trust Him to do even the impossible. He will not fail you.

9.

THE PROTECTION

"Thy rod and Thy staff they comfort me"

The trip through the "valley of the shadow of death" was not very pleasant. All along the way there was the constant danger of poisonous snakes and vicious animals waiting to devour their prey. But with careful vigilance the shepherd progressed cautiously through the cold, damp valley, prepared for any emergency.

The shepherd's armor consisted of his "rod." This was his weapon in the event of an attack. The rod was a club about two feet long, made from a small tree with the root end rounded off into a ball about the size of a man's fist. Into this the shepherd drove a number of spikes about two inches long. Usually one blow from the rod would kill or disable any foes. As the shepherd led his sheep through tall grass, he would swing the rod back and forth, left to right, to frighten away hiding enemies, thus preparing the way for the sheep.

Being a shepherd was not easy. On occasion he would suffer severe wounds in battling wild animals to protect his sheep. Examine any Palestinian shepherd. His hands and feet, especially, but other parts of his body as well, will be badly scarred from his skirmishes with wild animals. Sometimes a wolf would have a sheep in his mouth before the shepherd could get near. Soon there, the shepherd would swing his rod a mighty blow, crushing the head of the wolf. Instantly he would snatch the sheep from his captor and care for the wounds.

David as a young shepherd had rescued his sheep on many occasions. In fact he tells us about one incident in 1 Samuel 17:34-35, "And David said unto Saul, Thy servant kept his father's sheep, and there came a lion, and a bear, and took a lamb out of the flock: And I went out after him, and smote him, and delivered it out of his mouth: and when he arose against me, I caught him by his beard, and smote him, and slew him." David knew all about the shepherd's responsibilities in protecting his sheep while leading them through the precarious dark valleys. Now he says, "Yea, though I walk through the valley of the shadow of death. I will fear no evil: for Thou art with me; Thy rod and Thy staff they comfort me." Amidst the trials and conflicts of life David rests in the *protection* of his mighty Lord.

Consider our Great Shepherd and His abundant care for us. He fought the worst enemy ever known and won the battle. On the cross He suffered, bled, and died. Even more, He arose from the dead. Today He lives in His resurrected body at the right hand of the Father. Someday He will return to earth to rule and reign in power. His hands and feet are scarred. But He won the battle. As prophesied years before in

Genesis 3:15, the Lord Jesus bruised Satan's head. Christ delivered the crushing blow to the head of our worst enemy, the devil, providing eternal victory over the penalty and power of sin.

But you ask, "Doesn't the devil still live? What makes you think Christ won the victory?" In answer to the first question, let me say the devil is very much alive. Peter tells us, "the devil, as a roaring lion, walketh about, seeking whom he may devour" (1 Peter 5:8). He is far more subtle and dangerous than most of us realize. But through the Lord Jesus Christ the devil is a defeated foe. He may be mighty, but Christ is Almighty. The devil cannot harm any of the Lord's flock if we stay close to the Shepherd. We are assured that the Shepherd's "rod" will be our protection. He promises, "Because thou hast kept the word of My patience, I also will keep thee from the hour of temptation" (Revelation 3:10). This does not mean that we shall not be confronted by the enemy many, many times. But when he attacks, if we trust completely in Christ, we shall enjoy victory over the devil, saying, "Thanks be unto God, which always causeth us to triumph in Christ" (2 Corinthians 2:14).

It is regrettable to see so many defeated Christians. They are on the mountaintop today and in the valley tomorrow. First they are in Romans eight, and then back in chapter seven. Today they are in the promised land, tomorrow back in the wilderness. On they go, up and down, no stability, not knowing victory in

Christ. Oh, they are trying hard to overcome their besetting sin, but the weakness is, that they are "trying" instead of "trusting." We have a Great Shepherd who protects His sheep from all enemies. You say, "If only I could get the victory over this one thing, I could really count for Christ." You are a possessor of the victory. You need only claim it! Here it is in Romans 6:14, "Sin shall not have dominion over you." Grasp the truth. "Sin *shall not* have dominion over you." I am not talking about "sinless perfection" or the eradication or suppression of the old nature. Rather, I am speaking of daily, joyous, victorious Christian living in the power of Christ.

Major Whittle one time read the hymn, "I Need Thee Every Hour." "That will never do," he said. "I need Him every moment." Immediately he sat down and wrote the words to that inspiring hymn that has meant so much to us.

> Moment by moment I'm kept in His love;
> Moment by moment I've life from above;
> Looking to Jesus till glory doth shine;
> Moment by moment, O Lord, I am thine.

Victorious living is a moment-by-moment experience. There is no dedication experience great enough to last a lifetime. We need a daily experience with the Lord if we expect to overcome sin.

This is a supernatural walk. Self being crucified, it is a life of complete confidence in Christ. It is the walk of faith. Paul tells us in 1 Timothy 6:12 to "fight the good fight." But he does not end there. He hastens to add "of faith." To "fight the good fight" is a bitter struggle. To "fight the good fight of faith" is a glorious victory. We are told in James 4:7 to "resist the devil." If we do, the apostle says, "He will flee from you." How do we "resist" the devil? In our own strength, in the power of the flesh? Assuredly not! Those who try are always miserably defeated, for the devil strikes all the harder. The only possible way to defeat him is to do as James says in the first part of verse 7, "Submit yourselves therefore to God." This is the only way to defeat the devil. Get close to the Lord through a life of complete yieldedness and dependence. Peter expresses the same truth. After he tells about the devil's going about "seeking whom he may devour," he says, "whom resist steadfast *in the faith*." Faith is the victory. In 1 Corinthians 16:13 we are told to "stand fast in the faith." "To stand fast" does not mean to struggle. It means to trust implicitly in the Lord Jesus who can keep you from the struggle.

In the first chapter of Philippians we see Paul in prison for preaching the gospel. If ever he was discouraged, that should have been the time. But Paul was far from it. Throughout his brief Epistle to the Philippian saints we sense the keynote of joy and praise. He declares, "I have learned, in whatsoever state I am, therewith to be content" (Philippians 4:11). How did he learn this lesson? Surely not from his surroundings.

He sat in the shadow of possible martyrdom at any moment. What was the secret of this wonderful victory in the light of despair and gloom? The life of faith! Dependence on the Lord! Victory in Christ!

Christian, do you have this victory? Are you close by the side of your Lord, letting Him give you the victory over all temptations and evil? If so, then you can say with David, "Thy rod and thy staff they comfort me."

The rod was never used on the sheep but only on the enemy. The staff was used more directly in relationship to the sheep. The staff was a slender stick bent or hooked on one end. It provided several uses. While leading his sheep along unknown paths, the shepherd would tap on the ground with the staff to find the most solid ground. If the sheep should fall into a ravine, beyond the shepherd's reach, he would use his staff, twisting the hook into the wool of the sheep and lifting enough to enable him to climb out. Sometimes it was necessary to use it as a rod to correct the sheep. A tap on a back leg would usually bring him into position. At night as the sheep entered the door of the fold, the shepherd would use his staff to number the sheep. The staff was always used for the comfort or the well-being of the sheep.

Our Great Shepherd is not without His staff. It is so marvelous to know He always goes before us testing the ground on which we must walk. For the child of God there are really no accidents or uncertain paths. If we are truly following the Lord, we may be assured our entire way has been planned and prepared by Him. Of course, if we fail to follow Him, then we may encounter difficulty. But if we stay close by His side and "walk in the light as He is in the light" there can be no disappointments. All will be His appointments. To this end I must pray the Psalmist's prayer daily, "Make me to go in the path of Thy commandments; for therein do I delight" (Psalm 119:35).

Regrettably, we do not always follow our Lord. Sometimes our zeal tapers and the flame of passion for Christ burns low. We grow cold in heart. Prayer becomes a burden rather than a pleasure. Zest for Bible reading dwindles while zeal to win lost souls to Christ disappears. Occasionally every child of God drifts into these spiritual slumps. But praise God, He understands! His love will not let us go. Though we find ourselves wandering from His side, suddenly we feel the staff of His love tugging at our hearts. We hear His words, "I have loved thee with an everlasting love: therefore with lovingkindness have I drawn thee" (Jeremiah 31:3). We are so unworthy. But He reminds us that His love does not depend on our worthiness. We realize afresh that victory is in Him, not in our wayward hearts. "It is of the Lord's mercies that we are not consumed, because His compassions fail not. They are new every morning: great is Thy faithfulness" (Lamentations 3:22-23).

But suppose we refuse to hear His voice and neglect to answer the gentle touch of our Lord. Then He must be stern. The comforting staff becomes a rod of judgment. We must learn a new lesson. Affliction will be our teacher. Is God angry? Never is He angry with the believer! The same hand that chastens us is at the same time the hand that comforts us. Paul writes in 2 Corinthians 1:5, "For as the sufferings of Christ abound in us, so our consolation also aboundeth by Christ."

The Lord will not leave us in our affliction. He is with us every moment. He is preparing us to do His will instead of our own. Since believing on Him we are not our own, but His possession. "Ye are not your own," Paul says, "ye are bought with a price: therefore glorify God in your body, and in your spirit, which are God's" (1 Corinthians 6:19, 20). If we fail to glorify the Lord, then we will feel the touch of the rod; though remember, all affliction is for the believer's good and God's glory.

Could it be at this very moment you are feeling the touch of the Lord's rod? Remember that even this is another indication of His great love for you. "For whom the Lord loveth He chasteneth" (Hebrews 12:6). Don't revolt against your trial. Pray about it. Seek God's purpose in it. Claim the victory through Christ.

10.

THE PERIL

*"Thou preparest a table before me
in the presence of mine enemies"*

As the shepherd led his sheep over the long journey
to good, rich pasture land, he was confronted by many
dangers along the way. There was the constant dread
from above, as eagles and vultures swept down upon
the flock and stole the lambs. All around there were
unseen enemies in hiding. Ravenous beasts peered from
adjacent caves, waiting for their chance to attack.
Hyenas, jackals, wolves, and even lions were a constant
threat to the Palestinian shepherd and his sheep. Often,
little brown adders, living underground, came up to nip
the noses of the sheep as they grazed, producing death.
In addition to all this, thieves and robbers were a constant menace to the shepherd and his flock.

There were other *perils* to be encountered, but one
of the shepherd's greatest problems was the danger of
poisonous plants. The sky may be free of enemies.
Perfect calm may be all around. But mixed in the
luscious grass there may be a very dangerous enemy.
Poisonous plants, which are fatal to sheep, abound in

the Holy Land. Thus it is necessary for the shepherd to "prepare" the pasture. With his mattock in hand he begins the task. Grubbing out every noxious weed he finds, he lays them on little stone pyres to dry for burning. After much painstakingly hard work, the shepherd leads his sheep into the "prepared pasture" free from *perils* in the "presence" of their deadly plant enemies.

As the child of God follows his Great Shepherd over the pathways of life, he is plagued by many enemies, but the Shepherd never loses a sheep. The Lord Jesus says, "My sheep hear My voice, and I know them, and they follow Me: And I give unto them eternal life; and they shall never perish" (John 10:27-28). If we follow the Shepherd, we are secure from all enemies. To believe sincerely on the Lord Jesus Christ and to commit our lives to Him is to follow Him. For all who have faithfully done this, the Lord Jesus declares, "they shall never perish."

But you ask, "Is this all one need do to be assured of eternal life?" Absolutely! This is all you *can* do. For God says, "By grace are ye saved through faith; and that not of yourselves: it is the gift of God: Not of works, lest any man should boast" (Ephesians 2:8-9). The Lord Jesus offers salvation as a free gift to all who will believe on Him.

A missionary was going from bed to bed in a hospital, speaking with the patients about the Lord Jesus Christ. She came to an undersized and underdeveloped little boy, whose white face and emaciated form called forth her deepest sympathy. When she first talked to him about the Lord, he seemed to have little interest, but he became more and more concerned. He argued that he had attended church and thought this was sufficient. Prayerfully and carefully the missionary told him of our wonderful Lord Jesus who alone could save. She made other calls on this little fellow, but he was unwilling to make a commitment to Christ. One morning, however, when the missionary called, she found the boy beaming with new-found joy.

"What has happened?" she asked.

"Oh," he replied, "I always knew that Jesus was necessary; but I never knew until yesterday that He was enough!"

Praise God, He is enough! Would it not be wonderful if everyone could make this discovery? There are many who do not understand this fundamental truth of the Scriptures. It is not Christ plus good works, nor Christ plus the church, nor Christ plus the sacraments. It is Christ and He alone. We read in Acts 4:12, "Neither is there salvation in any other: for there is none other name under heaven given among men, whereby we must be saved." If you are in Christ you are saved. The Bible says, "Whosoever shall call upon the name of the Lord shall be saved" (Romans 10:13).

Because David knew the Great Shepherd he found the Lord to be sufficient for every occasion. "Thou preparest a table before me in the presence of my enemies," he says with confidence. David had encountered many enemies along life's way, but the Lord always gave deliverance. David wrote in Psalm 3:7, "Thou hast smitten all mine enemies." Like sheep, believers in Christ must face many enemies. Consider the eagles and vultures of the air ever swooping upon us, trying to snatch our "joy unspeakable" from us. Paul speaks in Ephesians 6:12 of the "spiritual wickedness in high places." The heavens are filled with invisible hosts of demons seeking to plague the child of God.

Not only are there enemies above. They are below as well. As a sheep might at any time be bitten by a snake underfoot, so you and I need to watch out for "that old serpent, called the Devil, and Satan, which deceiveth the whole world" (Revelation 12:9). He is "more subtil than any beast of the field" (Genesis 3:1). Ever ready to attack, he looks for an opportunity to instill the venomous poison of doubt.

Never forget it, child of God, Satan and all his demons are defeated in Christ. Though Satan is "the prince of this world" and "the God of this age," he is a defeated foe. Through the Holy Spirit who dwells in each believer, "the prince of this world is judged" (John 16:11). In the Holy Spirit's strength we may overcome Satan. The disciples overcame him when they cast out demons. This same power is our possession in Christ.

When Satan tempts us to doubt God, we should answer him from the Word of God like the Lord Jesus did. In tempting Christ, Satan offered sustenance without dependence, preservation apart from obedience, and glory without suffering. All was contrary to God's plan. To each temptation Jesus responded with a counter statement from the Scriptures. Through Christ we may meet Satan in the same victorious manner.

The story is told of the schoolboy who came to know the Lord Jesus through that wonderful verse John 5:24, "Verily, verily, I say unto you, He that heareth My word, and believeth on Him that sent Me, hath everlasting life, and shall not come into condemnation, but is passed from death unto life." When the boy arrived home, while sitting in the living room, he was tempted to doubt. He felt it was all a mistake. The temptation became so fierce that the boy thought Satan was actually under the chair talking to him. For a while the inexperienced lad did not know how to answer Satan, but then he got an idea. Quickly he reached for his Bible and turned to John 5:24. Pointing his finger to the verse he reached down under the chair as he said, "There you are, Satan, read it for yourself!" The boy in recounting the incident later said, "It seemed as if at that moment the devil disappeared." Satan cannot stand the Word of God.

Not only were the shepherd and his helpless sheep plagued by vultures and snakes. There was always the constant danger of thieves who lay in wait, ready to steal the sheep from the shepherd. This suggests to me the ungodly companions ever trying to turn the believer away from the Lord Jesus. How many broken hearts might have been spared had the Christian girl or boy obeyed God's eternal principle, "Be ye not unequally yoked together with unbelievers" (2 Corinthians 6:14). Many a testimony has been ruined because careless Christians were not prudent in choosing the kind of friends that pleased the Lord.

We need also to beware of the ravenous beasts that would seek to destroy the believer's joy. The Lord Jesus warned of the "false prophets, which come to you in sheep's clothing, but inwardly they are ravening wolves" (Matthew 7:15). These false teachers are on every hand seeking to deceive the children of God. Sometimes they appear as professors in our great institutions of higher learning or as velvet-mouthed orators in our pulpits. There is one test that can always distinguish the man of God and truth from the emissary of Satan and error. "What think ye of Christ?" (Matthew 22:42). How one answers this question will prove whether he is saved or lost. If Christ is merely a good man, a profound teacher, a wise leader, He is not the Christ of the Bible. The Christ of the Bible is the eternal Son of God, supernaturally born into this world to die for the sins of all who believe. To prove the efficacy of His sacrifice, He arose from the dead and now sits at the right hand of the Father until He comes again. Many there are who speak in the *name* of Christ. But "beware," they are "wolves in sheep's clothing."

The perils that confront the true believer are many, but to my mind there is one that exceeds them all. We spoke of the poisonous plants intermixed with the good grass. This brings to mind the noxious weed of "self" that endangers the usefulness of all believers. The Great Shepherd desires to pluck it out of our hearts, but we still feed upon its poisons. Probably you and I have no greater enemy.

A minister was asked one time, in a ministers' conference, "What is the chief problem of your work for God?" His straightforward and honest answer was, "Myself!" You and I have the same problem.

The Lord longs to fill us with Himself, but He cannot until we are emptied of ourselves. It was D. L. Moody who said, "Christ sends none away empty but those who are full of themselves." There has never been a selfish person in the world who was a great Christian.

What was the secret of Paul's mighty usefulness? It could all be summed up in one word, "selflessness." He was completely emptied of self. He had no interest in his own personal gain and comfort. "What things were gain to me, those I counted loss for Christ" (Philippians 3:7). He was not insistent on carrying out his own wishes and plans. He could say, "For to me to live is Christ" (Philippians 1:21). He was not supersensitive, touchy, and always insistent on having his own way. "Charity suffereth long, and is kind; charity envieth not; charity vaunteth not itself, is not puffed up, Doth not behave itself unseemly, seeketh not her own, is not easily provoked" (1 Corinthians 13:4-5). Paul was not given to blaming others; he searched out his own heart, declaring himself to be "the chief of sinners" (1 Timothy 1:15). Never did he boast of himself and his own works. He could say, "God forbid that I should glory, save in the cross of our Lord Jesus Christ" (Galatians 6:14). His basic interest and desire in life was summed up in Philippians 1:20, "So now also Christ shall be magnified in my body, whether it be by life, or by death." Oh, that God would put this earnest desire in our hearts.

If Christ were the supreme object in our lives, our enemies would quickly vanish under the mighty arm of our Great Shepherd. Christian, get close to Him. Eat of the "table" of blessing He has "prepared" for you in the midst of your "enemies."

11.

THE POWER

"Thou anointest my head with oil"

After a long eventful day, the sheep return to the fold. As they enter the door, single file, the shepherd quickly examines each sheep for briers in his wool or scratches or bruises. If needy sheep are found, they are removed from the line until the others have passed. The shepherd then gives his attention to the needy sheep. Each wound is carefully cleansed and then the shepherd dips his hand into a big earthen bowl of olive oil and anoints the wound. Thus the sheep are made comfortable and ready for a night of refreshing rest.

When David said of his Lord, "Thou anointest my head with oil," doubtless he was thinking of the many times Jehovah had ministered to him when he was tired in body and distressed in soul. But there is probably a deeper meaning. Oil in the Scriptures often symbolizes the Holy Spirit. Without the Spirit's power the believer's service for God is ineffectual and useless. David had found this to be the sad truth in his own life. He deeply sensed his own lack of power. In Psalm 6:2 he prayed, "Have mercy upon me, O Lord: for I am weak: O Lord, heal me; for my bones are vexed." But in the midst of his own weakness and frailty David found God's mighty power to be sufficient. In Psalm 59:16 he says, "But I will sing of Thy power; yea, I will sing aloud of Thy mercy." And in Psalm 62:11 he further says, "Power belongeth unto God."

It is this same truth we need to realize so greatly in our day, "Power belongeth unto God." Our churches are organized. We have well-planned and interesting programs. Our music is of the finest. Sermons are eloquent and scholarly. But why are not lost souls repenting and crying out to the living God for salvation? The figures show that church membership is at an all-time high. For many, however, joining church is considered to be on about the same plane as joining a lodge or a club. There is really no noticeable line of demarcation between the world and the church. We readily observe that many of our church people do the same things the unchurched do. Multitudes outside the church lie, cheat, drink cocktails, get divorces, and live immorally. But very often we observe church members doing the same things. There appears to be little transformation of life and character. Consequently the church is devoid of Holy Spirit power to win the lost to Christ.

In the apostolic days when one professed to be a follower of the Lord Jesus, it meant forsaking all to follow Christ. Oftentimes such complete surrender to the Lord resulted in ostracism from the fellowship of family and friends. Sometimes it even resulted in martyrdom. In our day however, it is quite popular for one to make a profession of faith in Christ and join the church. It gives position and prestige. It may even help one's business, opening the way for new contacts. But is this what God has intended for His Church? If we are to make an imprint in a world of sin with the gospel of Christ, like the shepherd's overflowing cup of oil our lives must overflow with the fullness of the Holy Spirit.

It is well to note that even the Lord Jesus performed all His mighty works in the strength and energy of the Holy Spirit. Recall how He began His ministry with the anointing of the Spirit. In Luke 4:18 we have the words of our Saviour concerning Himself, which were read in the synagogue at Nazareth on the Sabbath Day. This was a prophecy given by Isaiah many years before. "The Spirit of the Lord is upon Me, because He hath anointed Me to preach the gospel to the poor."

It is difficult for us to understand freely the relationship of the Son with the Holy Spirit in doing the work of the Father. One thing is obvious, however, from the verse just quoted. The Lord Jesus was definitely anointed and empowered by the Holy Spirit to carry on His ministry. In fact, He considered the Holy Spirit's work so sacred and important in His life that when He was accused by the Pharisees of healing in the power of the devil, He declared such action to be unpardonable. "Wherefore I say unto you, All manner of sin and blasphemy shall be forgiven unto men: but the blasphemy against the Holy Ghost shall not be for-given unto men" (Matthew 12:31-32). If the Lord Jesus gave such emphasis to the importance and recognition of the Holy Spirit's place in His ministry, certainly we, who are His followers, should give the Spirit the same respect in our hearts.

Perhaps it would be well to distinguish the "anointing" of the Spirit from two other scriptural terms, the "baptism" and the "fullness." The baptism of the Holy Spirit occurs the moment one believes on Christ. The repentant sinner is placed into the family of God to enjoy forever all the privileges and pleasures of union and communion with God. This truth is borne out in 1 Corinthians 12:13, "For by one Spirit are we all baptized into one body, whether we be Jews or Gentiles, whether we be bond or free; and have been all made to drink into one Spirit." Also at the time of conversion the believer is anointed by the Holy Spirit. The Spirit makes His abode in the believer, never to depart. This is a fulfillment of our Lord's words found in John 14:16, "I will pray the Father, and He shall give you another Comforter, that He may abide with you for ever." The "fullness" of the Holy Spirit has to do with the Spirit's control of the believer. One may be baptized and anointed by the Spirit, but sadly ineffectual in serving God, because of not being filled or con-trolled by the Spirit. God wants to do a mighty work through all Christians, but He can only do this to the extent to which they are committed to His control.

Without the fullness of God's power through the Spirit, believers accomplish little for the Lord. It is for this reason that God commands us, "Be filled with the Spirit" (Ephesians 5:18). We need not beg or plead for the fullness of the Spirit. Simply meet the requirements and the Spirit's fullness and power will be known. And what are the requirements? Just two: remove every obstacle and hindrance from the life and then receive the glorious promise by faith.

Dr. James H. McConkey used to tell of standing on the wall of a great dock. Outside was a huge lake vessel about to enter. At his feet lay the empty lock, waiting. For what? Waiting to be filled. Away beyond lay great Lake Superior with its limitless abundance of supply, also waiting. Waiting for what? Waiting for something to be done at the lock ere the great lake could pour in its fullness. In a moment it was done. The lockkeeper reached out his hand and touched a steel lever. A little wicket gate sprang open under the magic touch. At once the water began to boil and seethe. As it seethed, Dr. McConkey saw it rapidly creeping up the walls of the lock. In a few moments the lock was full. The great gates swung open and the huge ship floated into the lock now filled to the brim with the fullness.

What is this, but a picture of the great truth of the fullness of the Holy Spirit? Here are God's children like that empty lock, waiting to be filled. As that great inland sea outside the lock was willing and waiting to pour its abundance into the lock, so God is willing to pour His fullness into the lives of His children. But He is waiting. For what? Waiting as the lake waited, for something to be done by us. Waiting for us to reach forth and touch the lever of complete dedication to His will, thus opening the gates of our hearts through which abundant life and power shall flow and fill. God is ready and willing. Why wait? All the barriers and hindrances are on our side. We have the privilege of opening the door to His power. Christians, let us remove the obstacles. It may cost us our selfishness, pride, inconsistencies, and many other things. But whatever it is, it is well worth it. Let them go. Open the door. Receive God's fullness.

When one is filled with the Holy Spirit, the entire personality is affected. The fruit spoken of in Galatians 5:22-23 becomes obvious, not only to one's self, but to others. We shall see "love" that knows no bounds, "joy" that is unsurpassable, "peace" that cannot be disturbed, "longsuffering" that can suffer bitterness and, criticism, "gentleness" that can sympathize with others, "goodness" evidenced in clean living, "meekness" that can toil on without praise, "temperance" that knows how far to go and when and where to stop.

Greatest of all is the power for service. Jesus said in Acts 1:8, "Ye shall receive power, after that the Holy Ghost is come upon you: and ye shall be witnesses unto me." We are not filled merely to be happy, but to be useful. God never wastes or squanders His power.

The Spirit-filled man will be busy for God, seeking to lead lost souls to Christ.

Oh, if only those in our churches could sense the need of this power. Some do, but many do not. We have all the machinery, but we need the power. Here is a great newspaper press capable of turning out thousands of newspapers an hour. It is ready to begin its operation, but it lies silent and helpless, incapable of printing one paper. What is wrong? Throw the switch! Immediately contact is made, and the power thus released, rushes in, and the great press is alive with movement and power. In our day we number more church members than any previous age. Our churches are better off financially than ever before. We are deluged with new and improved media with which effectively to proclaim the gospel. But with all this results are deplorably few. What is wrong? We must throw the switch. God's power is stored up, ready to flow. Those of us who know the Lord must humble ourselves in His sight, cast out every obstacle, and be filled to overflowing for mighty usefulness.

What a potential we have in God's power! Yet most of us ignore it and fail to use it. God can pack an oak tree into an acorn. He can pack explosive power into an atom. His greatest power is in the gospel. He can take a worthless derelict like Jerry McCauley of the old Water Street Mission and transform him into a mighty evangel for the Lord. The gospel is still "the power of God unto salvation" (Romans 1:16). But to see this power unleashed it must be proclaimed through Spirit-filled men and women. There is nothing more pathetic than to see weak Christians trying to preach the living truth to dead sinners. Nothing could be more incongruous. How different was John Wesley's witness for Christ. Someone asked him how he got such crowds.

"I get on fire for God," he replied, "and then the people come to see me burn." Would to God that all across the world Christians were fiery hot for God, filled with His Holy Spirit power.

If you are a believer in Christ, you have been anointed with the Holy Spirit. You can say with David, "Thou anointest my head with oil." But are you filled with the Spirit? Is your life one of fruitfulness and usefulness for Christ? If not, surrender all to Him now. You know what is hindering God's power in your life. Let Him fill you as you yield your all to Him.

12.

THE PROVISION

"My cup runneth over"

Having completed his task at eventide, caring for the wounds of his sheep by cleansing them and anointing them with oil, the shepherd now provides for their thirst. In addition to the earthen bowl of olive oil, every sheepfold has a large cool stone jar of water from which the shepherd quenches the thirst of his sheep. In drawing his cup out of the jar, the shepherd never has it half or two-thirds full, but always overflowing and dripping. The sheep eagerly sinks his nose into the refreshing cup and drinks to his satisfaction.

In his days as a shepherd David had held the overflowing cup to his sheep many times. Now he declares of himself, "My cup runneth over." His overflowing cup was the one that never ran dry, the cup of the Lord's daily blessing. All who have believed in Christ have the privilege of drinking from this cup. Those outside of Christ can drink only from the cup of wrath. God tells us in Revelation 16:19 that they must drink of "the cup of the wine of the fierceness of His wrath." But to those who have trusted in God's Son for salvation, theirs is the blessed joy of drinking of all the blessings of the Lord: spiritual, material, and physical.

The wonderful truth is that God's blessings are always "overflowing." He not only promises to "pardon" us from our sins, but the Bible declares "He will abundantly pardon" (Isaiah 55:7). Not only is He "able to do" that for which we pray, but He "is able to do exceeding abundantly above all that we ask or think" (Ephesians 3:20). Not only do we have "joy" in following Christ, but "joy unspeakable and full of glory" (1 Peter 1:8). In Him we possess not only "peace," but "the peace of God which passeth all understanding" (Philippians 4:7). Indeed God "hath blessed us with all spiritual blessings in heavenly places in Christ" (Ephesians 1:3).

Christians should be the happiest people in the world because of God's gracious provision of the overflowing cup of blessing. We sing that old hymn "There *shall* be showers of blessing." Indeed there *are* showers of blessing falling on God's people constantly. How we ought to be praising Him for His wonderful love and care. David said in Psalm 107:8, "Oh that men would praise the Lord for His goodness, and for His wonderful works to the children of men!" Is it not true, however, that most of us grumble and complain more than we praise?

Perhaps you recall from the first few books of the Bible how God provided the overflowing cup of blessing for the children of Israel. What did they do? They murmured and complained because of impending dangers and lack of water and food. Nothing seemed to suit them. They became so disgruntled with everything and everybody that they seldom did anything else but give voice to their grievances. God was not happy about this. We read in Numbers 11:1, "And when the people complained, it displeased the Lord." When believers complain, it always displeases the Lord. Not only does it disturb all those around us, but it is a flat denial of God's abundant provision from His overflowing cup of blessing.

Some Christians are attacked by an occasional spell of complaining while others are always making a fuss about something. The acute complainer grumbles now and then under the pressure of some irritating circumstance. The chronic complainer grumbles under any circumstance. In fact, he never seems to be pleased. Usually he wants his own way. If he doesn't get it, he frets and whines. More and more his complaining becomes a habit, then a vice, rebelling against the grace and mercy of God.

The Lord Jesus came into the world that those who believe on Him "might have life, and that they might have it more abundantly" (John 10:10). J. B. Phillips translates these words of our Lord, "I came to bring them life, and far more life than before." New life in Christ should be a different kind of life. Indeed it is "far more life than before." Complaining and grumbling is of the old life. Believers possess new life in Christ.

Old things should be passing away, all things should be becoming new. The old sins of complaining and grumbling should be disappearing under the crimson flow of the blood of Christ. "Do all things," Paul says, "without murmurings and disputings" (Philippians 2:14).

In Psalm 33:1 David writes, "Rejoice in the Lord, O ye righteous: for praise is comely for the upright." Rejoicing and praise should be identifying marks of those who belong to the Lord.

How we need to master the truth of the last Psalm in the Bible. Though there are only six verses in Psalm 150, yet thirteen times the Lord exhorts us to praise Him. Some believers know very little about praising the Lord. God is extremely good and gracious to them, yet they never seem to acknowledge it. Repeatedly throughout the Word we are told to praise and thank God. In 1 Thessalonians 5:18 the apostle says, "*In* everything give thanks," and in Ephesians 5:20 he states "Giving thanks always *for* all things." This leaves no room for complaint, but only praise.

You may say, "You don't know what I have suffered." I don't have to know. All any of us needs to know is what God says in His Word. He knows what is best for each of us. He knows when to send the sunshine and when to permit the rain. Let us not even attempt to question His providence. Our Great Shepherd understands all about our problems and heartaches. Because of this He has promised to supply from His overflowing cup. To every believer He says, "Therefore I say unto you, Take no thought for your life, what ye shall eat, or what ye shall drink; nor yet for your body, what ye shall put on. Is not the life more than meat, and the body than raiment? Behold the fowls of the air; for they sow not, neither do they reap, nor gather into barns; yet your heavenly Father feedeth them. Are ye not much better than they?" (Matthew 6:25-26). If God cares for every need of all the little birds, flitting here and there, do you not think He will provide for you? Certainly He will! He knows of all your needs. He will supply.

Never forget the Lord Jesus is human, as well as divine. When He was born into this world He was clothed with a body of flesh. He is still in that body. He well understands all our weaknesses and frailties. The Oriental shepherd, even during warm days, would often don his fleece coat, and, when asked why, he would reply, "My sheep like to see me looking like themselves." Our Great Shepherd "took upon Him the form of a servant, and was made in the likeness of men" (Philippians 2:7), that He might identify Himself with all the problems of men. He sees them not only from the side of deity but humanity. He knows all about our heartaches and sorrows. That's why we can go to Him with everything, with the blessed assurance that He will abundantly provide from His overflowing cup.

Because one is a Christian is no assurance that he will not be confronted with numerous difficulties in life.

We shall have many burdens and trials. There is no home in the world so lowly that sorrow does not at some time enter the door. There is likewise no mansion so beautiful that sorrow does not mount its steps. Sorrow is the common lot of all. But the joy of being a Christian is that Christ knows all about our difficulties, and because of that, He will provide all the wisdom and help we need. What is sorrow, if the Lord Jesus walks by our side? Health may wither like a fading flower. Languor and disease may feed upon the frame. There may be tossings to and fro before the dawning of the day. Earthly friends may fail and forsake us. Death may bring desolation to our hearts and homes. But is the situation hopeless? Ah no! The Lord Jesus is the Great Shepherd. He well understands the sufferings of His sheep. He will provide. He will undertake. I need only do as He has said in His Word, "Trust in the Lord with all thine heart; and lean not unto thine own understanding. In all thy ways acknowledge Him, and He shall direct thy paths" (Proverbs 3:5-6). I must not worry, but trust Him in "all" my ways. My heart and mind must be reconciled to the fact of His all-sufficiency. Then I will hear the voice from behind saying, "This is the way, walk ye in it" (Isaiah 30:21). The way ahead may look very confusing, but the Lord cannot fail.

One day a little boy was lost. A policeman approached the crying lad and learning of his difficulty asked his address. The little fellow was able to tell the street and the number.

"That's easy," said the policeman. "Just go down this street three blocks. Then you will see a gas station. Turn left and go two blocks to a school. Turn right at the school. . . ." The policeman was interrupted by sobs.

"Why what is wrong?" he asked.

"I can't remember all of that," said the boy. "I am afraid I will never get home!"

The big policeman took hold of the little fellow's hand and said, "I will take you home. You do not need to know the way. I will guide you. Just trust me."

That is all the Lord Jesus asks us to do. Put your hand in His and trust Him. The future may seem dark and clouded, but there will be perfect light if you confidently follow Him. You may not be able to understand many things that come your way. It is not necessary that you do understand. God says, "Trust." Paul writes in 1 Timothy 4:10, "Therefore we both labour and suffer reproach, because we trust in the living God." Paul never asked God "why" or complained that he could not understand. He fully trusted the Lord.

I cannot understand
The why and wherefore of a thousand things;
The crosses, the annoyances, the daily stings,

I cannot understand—
But I can trust;
For perfect trusting, perfect comfort brings.

I cannot see the end,
The hidden meaning of each trial sent,
The pattern into which each tangled thread is bent,
I cannot see the end—
But I can trust;
And in God's changeless love I am content.

Are you content? Have you learned to drink from the all-sufficient satisfying cup of blessing held in the hand of our Great Shepherd? Paul could say, "I have learned, in whatsoever state I am, therewith to be content" (Philippians 4:11). God tells us in Hebrews 13:5, "Be content with such things as ye have." Then He adds, "I will never leave thee, nor forsake thee."

Here is the ground for the believer's contentment, the Unfailing Christ. Because of Him, "my cup runneth over." I have nothing to fear. He will care for every need, not only today, but every day. His cup never runs dry. It overflows with His abounding goodness. Are you one of His sheep? Do you know the Lord? If you do, then drink. Believe Him for all things.

13.

THE PERMANENCE

*"Surely goodness and mercy shall
follow me all the days of my life"*

In this wonderful Twenty-third Psalm David has led
us step by step along the daily path of the shepherd
and his sheep. As nightfall hastens on, the Psalmist sees
the sheep safely shut in the fold. He recalls how many
a night, after waiting until all the sheep were at rest,
he prepared to settle for his night's repose. Laying his
rod nearby in case of needed protection, he wrapped
himself in his heavy woolen robe and slept at the en-
trance to the fold. The whole picture is one of security.
It is very probable that with this in mind David declared,
"Surely goodness and mercy shall follow me all the days
of my life."

There were times when the sheep returned to the
fold at the close of the day and the shepherd discovered
that one of the lambs was missing. He quickly ascer-
tained which one it was, then calling one of the neigh-
boring shepherds to watch his sheep, he made quick
preparations to search for the lost. With his little lantern
he set forth in the darkness, calling and listening. As he

passed other shepherds he inquired about the missing sheep. Sometimes it was necessary to go only a short way, but then again he might find it necessary to retrace most of his day's journey. How happy the shepherd was when he finally heard the bleating of his lost sheep. Upon finding him he lifted him gently, laid him across his shoulders, and started for home. Along the way he would shout to fellow shepherds of whom he made inquiry, "Rejoice with me; for I have found my sheep which was lost." What joy he had in his heart to know the lost was found. This loving gesture on the part of the shepherd in seeking the lost sheep is but another evidence of "goodness and mercy" following the sheep all the days of his life.

Not only is the shepherd's goodness and mercy displayed at night as he seeks the stray sheep and keeps a protecting eye on those he has secured in the fold. He carefully watches over them during the daytime as well. As they traveled, the flock was protected, both front and back. The shepherd usually had two dogs to provide the watchful care from behind. Usually, if a sheep went astray or was hurt, the trained dogs barked and attracted the shepherd's attention. The two dogs, "goodness and mercy," were always alert to care for the sheep.

Those who belong to the Great Shepherd can say like David with confidence, "Surely goodness and mercy shall follow me all the days of my life." We are in the fold with our Great Shepherd watching over us. Sometimes, like sheep, we are disturbed by strange and unfamiliar noises. We cannot rest. Need we fear? "He that keepeth thee will not slumber. . . . The LORD shall preserve thee from all evil: He shall preserve thy soul. The LORD shall preserve thy going out and thy coming in from this time forth, and even for evermore" (Psalm 121:3, 7-8).

Sometimes we are prone to worry. We get our eyes on surroundings and off the Lord. Notice David does not say *possibly* or *maybe* "goodness and mercy shall follow me all the days of my life." He says "Surely"! There is not the slightest doubt in his mind. Where did David get this marvelous assurance? Through experience; he had put God to the test. This is why the Word of God was so real in his life. He said in Psalm 139:17, "How precious also are Thy thoughts unto me, O God! how great is the sum of them!" He searched the Word for the promises of the Lord and claimed them by faith. In Psalm 18:30 he says, "As for God, His way is perfect: the word of the Lord is tried: He is a buckler to all those that trust in Him." David had the blessed assurance that what God had promised He would also fulfill. "The Word of the Lord is tried," he says. You cannot convince David that the life of faith will not work. He knows differently. He had a living faith based upon the knowledge of the Scriptures, providing perfect peace for the future. In verses one to five of the Twenty-third Psalm David sums up the course of life's experiences. When he comes to verse six, looking back over the past and considering God's faithfulness, he seems to say, "Surely goodness and mercy will take care of the future as well."

There are times in our Christian experience when we fail to live a life of consecrated zeal and obedience to God. We stray thoughtlessly into the paths of sin. We forget all that the Lord has done for us. We neglect to trust in His "exceeding great and precious promises" (2 Peter 1:4). Praise God, His love does not rest upon our feeble faith. "Faithful is He that calleth you, who also will do it" (1 Thessalonians 5:24). My Great Shepherd will not stop loving me. Though my heart may become cold and indifferent, He will always be the same.

> O love that will not let me go,
> I rest my weary soul in Thee.

Can a mother stop loving her son? Of course not! Nor can God stop loving His own. Regardless of how wayward a child may be, rarely is there anything that will extinguish the flame of a mother's love. The story is told of a mother and her worthless son standing before a Christian judge awaiting the boy's sentencing. Many times before, the judge had tried to help the youth, but in vain. Finally he said, "I can do nothing more for this boy; I've done everything I can do. I give up. And I advise you, his mother, to do the same." The mother could not speak at first, but wiping the tears from her eyes she said, "Judge, I don't blame you.

You have been more than kind. You have gone out of your way to help us. I don't blame you for giving up. But, I can't give up this boy. I gave him life. I took care of him. I cannot go back on him. *He is mine!*" You may be sure God will do no less than a mother will do for her son. God's perfect love far exceeds the love of parents for their children. David said, "When my father and my mother forsake me, then the Lord will take me up" (Psalm 27:10).

We may wander from God but He will put "goodness" and "mercy" on our trail. Sometimes chastening may be necessary. It may even seem as though "goodness and mercy" have disappeared. Though often in disguise, they are there. God will never forsake His own. You need only turn around and you will find Him in His "goodness and mercy." "The goodness of God endureth forever" (Psalm 136:1). Have you wandered away from the Lord? Come back to Him. His "goodness" will receive you. His "mercy" will forgive you.

God's "goodness and mercy" are not temporary gifts. I am assured from the Twenty-third Psalm that they are my possessions until I meet Christ face-to-face. The benefits they provide are not for some days, but "all the days of my life." Nor does this mean only the sunny days, but dark as well. Whatever crosses the believer's path, be it sickness, death, unemployment, or a broken heart, "goodness and mercy" are there.

As the two shepherd dogs were always near to help

and protect, so God has placed "goodness and mercy" as divine watch dogs to preserve His sheep from all evil. Often they appear in the person of angels which God declares to be His "ministering spirits, sent forth to minister for them who shall be heirs of salvation" (Hebrews 1:14). Because of the presence of these divine messengers, we are never alone.

The ancient shepherds lived a very lonely life. During the summer months it was necessary to wander far afield to find subsistence for their flocks. For days and weeks they had no human companionship. But this isolation greatly increased the attachment of the shepherd to his sheep. They lived together with one common interest. They fought the same foes and looked forward with a unified hope for a safe return to the fold when the pilgrimage was over. This cemented their friendship and made them understand and enjoy each other all the more.

There are many lonely souls in the world. But those who know of the "goodness and mercy" of the Lord have a wonderful consolation in the fact that He knows all about loneliness. He went to Gethsemane alone. He went to the cross alone. He truly knows what it is to be completely forsaken. If you love Him, you are not alone. He is there. His "goodness and mercy" are there, "all the days of your life." The Lord goes "before" you to prepare the way. "When He putteth forth His own sheep, He goeth before them" (John 10:4). He is "round about" you in His daily protecting care.

"The angel of the Lord encampeth round about them that fear Him, and delivereth them" (Psalm 34:7). He is "underneath" you, upholding you with His arms of love. "The eternal God is thy refuge, and underneath are the everlasting arms" (Deuteronomy 33:27). He is "with" you and "in" you providing a constant supply of peace and comfort. "For He dwelleth with you, and shall be in you" (John 14:17). We are assured that "goodness and mercy" are "behind" and our Great Shepherd goes "before" to guard us from all danger. "Thou hast beset me behind and before, and laid Thine hand upon me" (Psalm 139:5).

What have you to fear, child of God? Why should you worry? God is unerringly concerned about you. Each individual believer is precious in His sight. This is expressed so vividly in the Twenty-third Psalm. Have you noticed the personal nature of the Psalm? It abounds in personal pronouns. Someone has called it the pronoun Psalm. The first person is referred to many times, as well as is the third person. How wonderful that as the believer reads each promise he may say, "Praise God! This is for me."

What do we need more than someone who is interested in our own personal problems? Wherever I go, I find that old and young alike have problems. Many of them are very serious and extremely distressing. David had problems, too. But he knew what to do with them. He rolled them on the Lord. To you and me he pleads with confidence, "Cast thy burden upon the Lord, and He shall sustain thee: He shall never suffer the righteous to be moved" (Psalm 55:22). Never? No, never! "Goodness and mercy shall follow me all the days of my life."

> All things are possible to Thee,
>   Oh, Lord, we know it's true;
> The little things we cannot see,
>   The things we cannot do,
> Oh, praise Your Name, are easily done
>   With little pain or fret.
> You help us gain, the battles won,
>   You have not failed us yet.
> It's we who fail to do our best—
> It's we who do not meet the test.
>
> We look at things and groan and say,
>   "I can't go through, I'll fall,"
> But oh, You help us to obey—
>   Help us to conquer all.
> You give us strength in time of need,
>   Encouragement in grief;
> And sometimes, You from Heaven feed
>   Our hungry souls, and bring relief.
> It's we who take our hand from Thine,
> We cannot blame Your Name Divine.
>
> You take us over rocky roads,
>   You pull us from the mire;
> But oh, You take away the load
>   And help us to go higher.
> We thank You for each task, each tear,

For things that weren't so nice to do,
Because the times that seemed so queer,
    Are just the times You took us through.
We thank You, Lord, for victories won,
But oh, we know You've just begun!

14.

THE PROSPECT

*"And I will dwell in the house
of the Lord for ever"*

David closes the Prince of Psalms with a clear-cut statement about his *prospect* for the future. With the exception of verse one, he has been telling of God's immediate and present care. In concluding he assures us that all the security he has enjoyed thus far will continue throughout eternity, "And I will dwell in the house of the LORD forever."

So often this statement refers to the believer's heavenly home. Indeed it does look forward to our future state of blessedness in the presence of the Lord. But it is also intended to be a present experience. Heaven begins the moment we are born into the family of God by faith in Christ. Daily, as we live in fellowship with Him, we enjoy the wonderful foretaste of the future glory that shall be ours in Heaven.

Notice that David does not say, "Surely goodness and mercy shall follow me all the days of my life:" and *then* "I will dwell in the house of the LORD for ever." As "the goodness and mercy" of the Lord follow him, he is already dwelling "in the house of the Lord." In Psalm 27:4 he writes, "One thing have I desired of the LORD, that will I seek after; that I may dwell in the house of the LORD all the days of my life, to behold the beauty of the LORD, and to enquire in His temple." In this passage he states the paramount desire of his heart. This was not merely a prospect for the future, but a possession for the present. David desired to live in the presence of the Lord continually. This should be the earnest longing in every redeemed heart. We are to live not only with the prospect of Heaven, but in its present reality. Those who belong to Christ should walk with Him beholding "the beauty of the Lord" in a life of submission and yieldedness to His will. This is the really happy life. The believer's most consuming passion should be to live in joyful, unbroken fellowship with the Father and with His Son through the guidance and leadership of the Holy Spirit. Here and now we should be enjoying this wonderful fellowship which we shall further enjoy throughout eternity. The riches of God's marvelous grace, the wonders of His love, the greatness of His wisdom, the grandeur of His power, and the surpassing majesty of His glory are all our possessions now in the invincible Christ.

How may the child of God really know all these blessings? There is only one way. Let the Lord Jesus have absolute and complete control of the entire life. The self-made life is ineffectual for the Lord. He desires the God-planned life. If He is to lead and direct our lives, there must be a will on our part to permit Him to have the right of way in our hearts. This may not be easy. But if you are ready, God will do the rest; you will find victory and blessing as you "dwell in the house of the Lord" now, with an even greater prospect for the future.

In the city of St. Louis, a new highway is under construction. Vast areas are being cleared through the residential sections. Scores of homes have been demolished. Business people driving to and from work are inconvenienced by detours and traffic jams. The peace and serenity of neighborhoods has been disrupted. Familiar landmarks have disappeared. This area will never be the same. The whole project is destructive, disturbing, and expensive. Were this all to be realized from this tremendous sacrifice, it would be extremely hopeless. But think of the finished product, the new highway. Consider the convenience it will be for untold thousands for years to come. It is burdensome now, but highways cannot be constructed in any other way.

Nor is it easy to give God the right of way to our hearts. When we do, it is so wonderful! It is blessed! It is thrilling! In fact there is nothing more enjoyable in life than to live each day walking in fellowship with the Lord.

One time a happy Christian exclaimed to a brother in the faith, "It's a grand thing to be saved!"

"Indeed it is," replied the friend, "but I know something better than that."

"Better than being saved?" asked the puzzled Christian. "What can possibly be better than that?"

"The fellowship of the One who saved me," was the reply.

Actually is there anything better than living day by day in harmony with God, doing His will, hating sin, and obeying Him? Many make a profession of faith, but beyond that they fail to advance. The old sins and idols are carried over into the new life without any noticeable change or transformation. There seems to be little interest in doing what God wants, in forsaking and in denouncing sin. We read in Colossians 3:1-3, "If ye then be risen with Christ, seek those things which are above, where Christ sitteth on the right hand of God. Set your affection on things above, not on things on the earth. For ye are dead, and your life is hid with Christ in God." This is not to suggest that we are to become so heavenly that we are of no earthly value. It does mean that the Lord Jesus should have the preeminence in all that we do or say. It is to exclude from the life anything and all that displeases the Lord.

Those who live in the "house of the Lord" are those who experience the joy of the Lord. In Psalm 16:11 David speaks of the "fullness of joy" known only to believers who are walking with God. "Thou wilt show me the path of life; in Thy presence is fullness of joy; at Thy right hand there are pleasures for evermore."

Many Christians have never known this "fullness of joy" because of an unsurrendered heart and will. In Ephesians 3:19 Paul prays that the saints at Ephesus "might be filled with all the fulness of God." Paul knew that with "the fullness of God" comes the "fullness of joy." As we empty ourselves of every hindrance, and in humble commitment yield to the fullness of Christ, we shall abound in His marvelous joy. The only thing that prevents us from knowing this life of blessedness at this very moment, is the failure to surrender everything to Christ.

Suppose two young people are planning to be married. Several weeks before the wedding day, the young man informs his bride-to-be that he has a surprise for her. They take a short drive together and stop in front of a lovely new home. He turns and says, "Here is our house. I had it built just for us." She is practically speechless as she gazes in wonder at this marvelous surprise. In a few moments they enter and look at each room together. Having seen all the rooms and closets, the young lady recalls that there was one closed door. She inquires about it.

"Oh," says her lover, "you must never go in there. That is mine. The entire house is yours with the exception of that one room. You will never be allowed in there." How do you think she would feel? Her joyfulness would be clouded very quickly, would it not? Unless there were a change, I doubt that she would even go through with the marriage.

It is doubtful that one contemplating marriage would do such a thing, but do not many Christians treat God in this manner? Reserving a little room of the heart for self and sin, they say, "Lord, you can have everything with the exception of this one little room. That is mine." Until the door to that secret chamber is opened and God is given full possession of the heart, it is impossible to know blessing and victory in the Lord. Christian, do you know of anything in your life that displeases God? Claim the victory immediately. Call on the Lord and ask Him to clean out every corner of your heart that you may know the fullness of God's blessing.

It is wonderful to "dwell in the house of the Lord" now, but oh, the greater joy that will be ours when we dwell there "forever" in the presence of Christ. When David said "forever," he must have been thinking of his shepherd days. To have a home "forever" was a coveted possession for a shepherd. Most of them lived in tents. Their nomadic life demanded that as soon as the sheep consumed the pasture in any section, the tents had to be moved to a fresh pasture. David rejoices to know that soon he would be in his eternal home "forever" in the presence of the Lord. To every child of God the Bible declares, "For we know that if our earthly house of this tabernacle were dissolved, we have a building of God, an house not made with hands, eternal in the heavens" (2 Corinthians 5:1). The Lord Jesus expressed a similar truth in John 14:2 when

He said, "In My Father's house are many mansions [abiding places]: if it were not so, I would have told you. I go to prepare a place for you." Adequate space for large families was always a problem in the Eastern homes. But in the "place" our Lord went to "prepare" there will be plenty of room for those who enter. It is marvelous to know God has prepared the place and that after this life has ended, those who know Him go to be with Him. What a day of rejoicing and blessing it will be when we come into the full meaning of David's words, "I shall dwell in the House of the Lord for ever."

As we draw to the close of these messages on the Twenty-third Psalm, let us look once again to the key that unlocks the door to all the promises presented in the Psalm, "The LORD is *my* Shepherd." There is no other way to "dwell in the house of the Lord for ever" other than the way God has prescribed, in allowing the Lord Jesus to be our Shepherd. The Twenty-third Psalm is meaningless until Christ is received as Lord. You may have some knowledge of the Psalm and the shepherd customs, but most important of all is to know the Shepherd personally and to be able to say "the Lord is *my* Shepherd."

Among the guests present at a house party were an actor and a saintly old minister. The actor was requested to give a recitation. He consented, and asked what the guests would like. The Twenty-third Psalm was suggested. With perfect diction and clear resonant voice he recited the Psalm, much to the admiration of his hearers. They applauded loudly. Then someone suggested that the minister recite the Psalm. At first he refused, but upon being urged, he closed the Bible and in reverent voice with deep feeling he slowly repeated the familiar verses. His audience realized he was not reciting something merely memorized, but he was telling of his own experiences with the Shepherd he loved.

There was no applause after he finished. A solemn hush fell upon the enraptured audience. After a few moments of silence, the actor went to the minister, took his hand and said, "Sir, I know only the Psalm; you know the Shepherd."

How about you dear friend? Do you know the Psalm, but not the Shepherd? If you do not know the Lord Jesus Christ, invite Him into your life. The Twenty-third Psalm will immediately become more than beautiful sounding phrases. It will be a source of refreshing and endless hope in Him who is our Great Shepherd.